£4

Helen Hempster

Hay 2003

CONFESSION

By the same author:

MARRIAGE AND CELIBACY (SCM Press)

CONSECRATION OF THE LAYMAN (Helicon Press)

THE EUCHARISTIC MEMORIAL (Lutterworth Press; John Knox Press)

MODERN MAN AND SPIRITUAL LIFE (Lutterworth Press; World Christian Books)

MARY, MOTHER OF THE LORD, FIGURE OF THE CHURCH (Faith Press, now Mowbray; Herder and Herder)

REVELATION (Newman Press)

VISIBLE UNITY AND TRADITION (Darton, Longman and Todd; Helicon Press)

OUR FAITH – BASIC CHRISTIAN BELIEF (Mowbray)

EUCHARIST AT TAIZÉ (Faith Press, now Mowbray)

PRIESTHOOD AND MINISTRY (Mowbray)

THE MYSTERY OF THE EUCHARIST (Mowbray)

Confession

MAX THURIAN
Brother of Taizé

MOWBRAY
LONDON & OXFORD

Copyright © Les Presses de Taizé 1985
ISBN 0 264 67047 7

(First English edition published 1958 by SCM in their Ministry
and Worship series edited by Professor G. W. H. Lampe.)

Translated by Edwin Hudson from the French LA CONFESSION,
Delachoux & Niestlé S.A., Neuchâtel, Switzerland, 1953.

This revised edition, with new Foreword, published 1985
by A. R. Mowbray & Co. Ltd,
Saint Thomas House, Becket Street,
Oxford OX1 1SJ

Printed in Great Britain by Biddles Ltd, Guildford

British Library Cataloguing in Publication Data
Thurian, Max
   Confession. — Rev. ed.
   1. Penance   2. Sacraments — Catholic Church
   I. Title   II. La Confession. *English*
   265′.6   BX2260

ISBN 0–264–67047–7

TO BROTHER ROGER
PRIOR OF TAIZÉ
WHO TRAINED ME IN THE MINISTRY OF
THE CURE OF SOULS

CONTENTS

FOREWORD
(*to this revised edition*)

The Taizé Community, which, when it began, was by many
Protestants regarded as a daring and dangerous experiment, has
become known and honoured throughout the Christian world.
From the start it was a community of reconciliation, a group of
Reformed pastors and others seeking to bridge the great gulf
between Protestants and Catholics by a reaffirmation of authentic Christian praxis. This included the rediscovery of certain
Catholic elements in Protestantism, which the Reformers did
not, as may be supposed abandon, but criticized and restated,
though in the long centuries of separation and hostility, they may
have been lost. One is the centrality of the Eucharist; another,
the practice of Confession.

In this book, Brother Max Thurian, a leading theologian of
Taizé, gives a precise account of the Protestant critique of the
Sacrament of Penance, and shows how Luther and Calvin, in
their different ways, attacked its scholastic formalism and
superstitious quasi-magic. But the former exulted in its joyous
and liberating discipline, the living out of Baptism, and the latter
saw it as a proper and beneficent adjunct to preaching and
spiritual counsel, 'a useful aid to those who need it', and have the
faith, though small as a grain of mustard seed, to receive
absolution, through the merits of Christ. Thurian then gives a
history of the practice and shows that it is part of any vital belief
in the communion of saints. One of the most important – and
most criticized – chapters concerns the relation of Confession to
Psycho-analysis in which the author wrestles with the fact that
the saints have not generally been men and women of psychological equilibrium, and yet have not wallowed in those
pathological states which it is the task of the psycho-analyst to

identify and where partnership with him may be of great help to pastor and penitent alike. The cure, however, is likely to demand spiritual ministry, the invocation of God the Holy Spirit and the application of the promises of the gospel. The roles of pastor and analyst must remain distinct. The book is full of wise advice and penetrating practical discussions, such as that of the traditional distinction between mortal and venial sin, which Thurian rightly opposes, though he concludes by saying, *mutatis mutandis* with Calvin that 'all sins are both mortal and venial: mortal because they merit death, venial because all can be pardoned.'

It was fashionable in the decade after this book was first published, to declare that the great difference between congregations then and in the earlier years of the century was the difference between a sense of guilt and a sense of doubt. This contention came from some who had long experience of Christian advocacy. The task of commending the gospel has not been made easier by the corrosion of doubt, which has eaten into many of our contemporaries and rusted the faculties of faith. But no one engaged in pastoral ministry today can deny that thousands of people are enslaved by guilt of real or imagined offences, and need the word of absolution and release. This should be pronounced in every sermon, as it is in the blessed sacrament of the Table; but it often needs to be conveyed also in the private acts of a soul friend, usually ordained to the ministry of word and sacrament, who thereby serves as a priest of the most high God. For such this book will continue to be of very great help.

GORDON S. WAKEFIELD

PREFACE

PROTESTANTS should be grateful to Pastor Max Thurian for putting before them, in the pages which follow, the problem of confession. That 'Protestants do not go to confession' is one of the chief elements in the popular definition of 'Protestantism'. It must be allowed that, apart from a few exceptions, the definition is in conformity with the facts. Many of our church members are extremely surprised when they discover that our pastors, at their consecration or ordination, undertake to 'keep secret to themselves those confessions which may be made to them for the quieting of conscience'.

Is there any justification in the teaching of Holy Scripture for the departure from the practice of confession on the part of the majority of the Reformed Churches? Does it compromise the development of the Christian life or not? Pastor Thurian constrains us to ask ourselves these questions. Those who read what he has to say will no longer find it possible to dismiss with a curt negative the question of whether the Christian ought normally to practice confession. To be sure, they may not find themselves in complete agreement with every argument put forward by the author, but they will no longer be free to ignore the fact that this is a problem of Christian thought and life whose solution must be courageously sought.

I warmly commend Pastor Thurian for reminding us at the outset of his study of Calvin's admirable words on the subject of confession. The scriptural foundation on which the Reformer's thought—and, following him, that of our author—is based, is at once made clear. One cannot excise from the New Testament James' teaching on the subject of mutual confession, nor, above all, the words of Christ concerning absolution. It is possible to dispute the way in which Calvin does in fact reserve to the 'ministers ordained' by the Church the task of hearing the confessions

13

of the faithful and of assuring them, where appropriate, of the forgiveness of their sins. But even so one cannot but acknowledge the vigour of his thought and the penetrating power of his argument.

Pastor Thurian does not of course restrict himself to prefacing his book with a few pages from Calvin. He takes up again the essential points of Calvin's teaching on the subject, adding to them the teaching of Luther, and recalling the very clear doctrine concerning confession set forth in the latter's Great and Little Catechisms. Indeed, when we see the views the Reformers held, we wonder how it is that the Protestant Churches should have been so unfaithful to them on this point!

It would seem that this is one of the baneful consequences of what we call Protestant individualism, whose excesses have done so much harm. But why is it that this individualism has triumphed so easily, particularly in Reformed Protestantism, not only over the sense of the Church as a community, but also over the instructions given by Christ to his Apostles—to the Church, therefore—concerning the forgiveness of sins? Certainly the historical circumstances surrounding the first two and a half centuries of the life of the Reformed Churches were no strangers to these things. It is nevertheless true that a necessary but excessive reaction against the distortions, abuses, and the pernicious effects of confession as it was too often practised in the Roman Church did result in the faithful being deprived of a means of grace which, if used freely and intelligently, would no doubt have borne much spiritual fruit in the life of our Churches.

Pastor Thurian's study is therefore rendering a very great service in bringing us back to the teaching of the Reformers and of the New Testament. He is, moreover, careful to warn us against the danger of sacramental magic. The relationship between Word and Sacrament is insisted upon, as also that between Faith and Sacrament. 'It is always faith which God answers in the sacrament.'[1] There can be no room at all, on the basis of the revelation given by Holy Writ, for the *opus operatum*.

[1] p. 57.

So far so good! But is confession, or more exactly, the absolution given to the Christian who has confessed, a sacrament? That it is, Pastor Thurian asserts in terms that will not fail to give rise to serious reservations in many quarters. I myself came up against this many years ago when, in a meeting of the *Amis de la Pensée protestante*, I maintained on the basis of the teaching of Melanchthon that absolution is a sacrament.[1] The opponents of this thesis admittedly find support for their claim in the abandonment by Luther of his original position (to which Melanchthon remained faithful), and the uncertainty of Calvin on the point. The really important thing is to know exactly what it was that Christ gave to his Church when he remitted to his Apostles the power of binding and loosing. It will be very interesting to compare the interpretation given by the present author with the exegesis of the texts studied by Pastor Thurian given by Oscar Cullmann in his important work on the Apostle Peter.

I have just spoken of 'reservations'. I imagine that they will be most strongly aroused by Chapter V, 'Confession and Psychoanalysis'. May one hope that these pages will be the starting-point of a thorough discussion of what assistance, if any, psychoanalysis may bring to those entrusted with the task of spiritual direction, and what collaboration, if any, there ought to be between the psychoanalyst and the confessor?

Pastor Thurian expresses the hope that 'the consideration of the unfortunate effects of psychoanalysis on the faith of believers in certain cases will not lead to a hardening of the Church's attitude to that science'. He himself points to a danger which he calls 'psychologism', whose theological consequences are likely to be 'a certain dogmatic relativism and a certain moral complacency'. This somewhat nicely-expressed judgement does not prevent the author from recognizing that the fears that have been expressed are 'not without foundation' and that 'vigilant attention' is indispensable.

[1] 'Y a-t-il d'autres sacrements que le Baptême et la Cène?', in *Foi et Vie*, January, 1934.

No one, I think, denies the important place that has been won over the last half century or so by psychoanalysis. It is nevertheless permissible to ask whether no less positive results have not been obtained by other 'psychological' methods. Of these it seems that Pastor Thurian takes no account at all and that for truly pathological cases he considers analysis to be indispensable.

But if it is in these cases only[1] that psychoanalysis ought to intervene, is it necessary to deal with it at such length? The impression is given that pastors are advised in certain cases to urge the parishioners whose confessors or spiritual directors they are (and the two functions are quite different) to have recourse to analysis. But how many psychoanalysts are there whose faith —Protestant or Catholic—gives them a *Christian view* of the man or woman whom they are analysing? I cannot refrain from adding also: how many members of our Churches are in a position to shoulder the expense of a *complete analysis*, made by a psychoanalyst who inspires the necessary confidence?

Pastor Thurian relies on analysis to give certain types of ascetic 'an equilibrium in Christian obedience more in conformity with the Gospel'. But he thereupon counsels prudence, 'for it would be disastrous if a psychological analysis . . . were to turn a saint into a healthy animal'.[2] 'What,' he asks, 'would be the result of psychoanalysing a Francis of Assisi?' Or, one might add, a St Paul? One shudders to think of the outrages that might be perpetrated against saintliness by psychoanalysts for whom terms such as sin, repentance, faith, and Christian love stand for nothing more than psychic phenomena.

Howbeit, neither spiritual direction nor confession are in any danger of being ousted by psychoanalysis. Both answer deep and permanent needs of the Christian soul. Not to recognize their necessity and their value is to condemn oneself to an impoverishment of spiritual life. Their practice in the charity and respect for liberty with which they are informed by grace opens to them

[1] p. 83.   [2] p. 95.

wonderful possibilities of growth in the 'life in Christ'. This is made penetratingly clear by Pastor Thurian's study. Every reader of this book will be grateful to the author for obliging him to lay bare his life before God and to ask himself if in not using spiritual direction or confession and absolution he has not been neglecting a great means of grace, offered by a merciful Love of which it is the Church's duty to be the permanent witness to us.

MARC BOEGNER

CALVIN'S TEACHING ON CONFESSION

'MOREOVER [apart from confession to God], the Scripture sanctions two kinds of private confession; one to be made for our own sake, which is referred to in the direction of St James, that we should "confess our faults one to another" (James 5.16); for he means that, revealing our infirmities to one another, we should assist each other with mutual advice and consolation; the other, which is to be made for the love of our neighbour, to pacify and reconcile him to us, if we have done him any injury. In the former species of confession, though the Scripture, by not expressly appointing any one to whom we should disburden ourselves, leaves us at liberty to confess to any member of the Church who shall appear most suitable; yet, since the Pastors must be considered more proper for this than others, we ought chiefly to make choice of them. I say that they are more suitable than others, since, in their very vocation to the ministry, they are designated by God, to instruct us to subdue and correct our sins, and to certify us of God's goodness, for our consolation. For though the office of mutual admonition is committed to all Christians, yet it is especially confided to ministers. And so, while we all ought mutually to console each other, yet we see that *ministers are constituted by God witnesses and as it were sureties, to certify our consciences of the remission of sins*; insomuch that *they themselves are said to remit sins and loose souls* (Matt. 16.19; 18.18; John 20.23). *When we find this attributed to them, let us consider that it is for our benefit.*

'Therefore, let every believer remember, if he feels such secret anguish from a sense of his sins, that he cannot find repose without some exterior aid, to use this remedy, as it is offered him by God: which is, that in order to alleviate his distress, he should first disburden himself to his pastor, whose office it is, both publicly and privately, to comfort the people of God with the doctrine of the Gospel. But we should always be careful to lay no yoke on the conscience, where God has given no positive command. Hence it follows that such confession ought to be free, so as not to be exacted of any, but only to be recommended as a useful aid to those who need it. It follows also that they who freely practise it on account of their need of it, should neither be compelled by any precept, nor be induced by any artifice, to enumerate all their sins; but only so far as they shall think expedient, that they may receive solid consolation. Good and faithful pastors ought not only to leave the Church in possession of this liberty, but also to defend it with all their power, if they wish to preserve their ministry in purity without tyranny, and the people from superstition. . . .

'But that the sheep should present themselves to their pastor, whenever they desire to partake of the Supper, I am so far from opposing, that *I earnestly wish it were universally observed*. For those who experience distress of conscience may use this opportunity to their consolation; and the Pastor will be afforded an opening and means to admonish those who require it; provided that care be always taken to guard against tyranny and superstition.

'In all these three kinds of confession *the power of the keys is exercised*: either when the Church implores pardon by a solemn acknowledgement of its transgressions; or when an individual, who, by any remarkable crime, has occasioned an offence to the Church, declares his repentance; or when he who needs the assistance of the minister on account of the disquietude of his conscience, discloses his infirmity to him. . . .

'When the whole congregation stands, as it were, before the judgement seat of God, when they confess themselves guilty, and acknowledge that they have no refuge but in the mercy of God, it is no trivial consolation to have *Christ's ambassador* present, furnished with the mandate of absolution, by whom they may have their *absolution pronounced in the name of his Master, and by his authority*. Here we see how great is the value and the advantage to us of the use of the keys, when this *embassy of reconciliation* is rightly performed, with becoming order and reverence. So, when he who had alienated himself from the Church is restored to the unity of the brethren, and obtains pardon from the Church, how great a blessing does he experience in seeing that he obtains forgiveness from them to whom Christ has said, "Whose soever sins ye shall remit on earth, they shall be remitted in heaven" (Matt. 18.18; John 20.23).

'Nor *is private absolution less efficacious or beneficial*, when it is used by those who need relief of conscience. For it sometimes happens, that he who hears the general promises of God, which are addressed to the whole Church, nevertheless remains in some suspense, and is still *disquieted with doubts as to the forgiveness of his sins*. But *if he discloses secretly to his Pastor his distress*, and hears the Pastor applying *to him in particular* the general doctrine, he will be *straightly assured* where formerly he was in doubt, and will be *liberated from every trepidation, and find repose of conscience*. . . . Nevertheless when we are treating of the power of the keys, we must always be cautious not to imagine given to the Church any power that is divorced from the preaching of the Gospel.'[1]

*　　　　*　　　　*

'I like the Protestant religion, because the priests get married and one does not have to go to confession. . . .'

How often we have heard some such expression of opinion from the lips of lapsed or indifferent Roman Catholics, convinced that they were thus describing all that is original in Protestantism!

In this way the Reformed Church is taken to be a community in which each member is responsible for his own conscience, and is answerable for his conduct to nobody except to God. This is a

---

[1] John Calvin, *Institutes of the Christian Religion*, edition of 1560, Bk. III, Ch. IV, Paras. 12, 13, and 14, passim. (Translator's note: The most recent French edition is that published in 1888 by Béroud, Paris. In English, the standard translation made in the last century by John Allen, and republished in 1935 and 1958 by James Clarke & Co., London, needs revision and should be read with reserve.)

judgement as shallow as the ignorance from which it proceeds is profound. The sixteenth-century Reformers, and after them the Lutheran and Reformed Churches, asserted that the practice of confession was both well-founded and profitable. Pastors at their consecration still promise to 'keep secret those confessions which may be made for the quieting of conscience'.[1]

It is necessary, however, to point out the modifications to which the Protestant tradition subjected the Roman Catholic doctrine of the sacrament of penance, and to admit that the practice of true confession in accordance with the teaching of the Gospel has been gradually lost. It has given place to 'soul-healing', a kind of spiritual direction, or to 'sharing', a sort of reciprocal release. There is afoot today a strong movement towards the rediscovery of the true meaning and practice of confession.

[1] *Liturgie de Genève*, 1945, p. 345.

CHAPTER ONE

PROTESTANT CRITICISM OF THE SACRAMENT OF PENANCE[1]

LUTHER'S criticism of the sacrament is theologically in line of succession from the Franciscan school, and, more particularly, from Duns Scotus. St Thomas Aquinas had very clearly laid down the three parts of penance as essential to the sacrament, the matter, as it were, (*quasi materia*) of the sacrament: contrition of the heart —sorrow for having committed sin and determination not to fall into it again; spoken confession—a complete avowal to one and the same priest of all the sins one remembers; satisfaction—acts of reparation proposed by the priest, mainly fasting, prayer, and alms-giving. The form of the sacrament he held to consist in the words of absolution (*Ego te absolvo*) pronounced by the priest, the minister of the sacrament, and its effect was the absolving of the sin.[2] The Council of Florence, in 1439, in its decree concerning the Armenians,[3] merely took up once more the Thomist doctrine, which remains today the official belief of the Roman Church.

Another doctrinal current made its appearance in the Middle Ages, Duns Scotus being its outstanding exponent. He taught that the acts of the penitent—contrition, confession, satisfaction— though integral, are not essential parts of the sacrament of penance.

---

[1] The reader who is interested only in the problem and the practice of confession may omit this chapter. In any case I have kept the historical and critical element to a minimum, my first and chief aim being to help the ordinary church member.

[2] *De fidei articulis et septem sacrementes*, ed. Mandonnet, *Opuscula omnia S. Thomae*, Vol. III, Paris, 1927, p. 16.

[3] *Dictionnaire de Théologie catholique*, ed. Vacant & Mangenot, Letouzey & Ané, Paris, 1903, Vol. XII, Col. 1046-7.

The only essential is the absolution in respect of the sins, the three acts of penitence being only the signs of it.[1] Furthermore, he understood the efficacy of the sacrament in the sense of a remission of the fault and of the penalty. The forgiveness of sins does not result immediately from absolution; absolution provokes a certain disposition, and it is this disposition which, through God's promise, calls forth forgiveness.

Concerning contrition, he shows that there exist two ways of justification (in the scholastic sense): one, contrition (superior attrition), can dispense with the sacrament; the other, attrition, suffices for the remission of sins in the sacrament. In connection with the discipline of confession he is less strict concerning its obligatory nature, holding that it is obligatory, by divine precept, only in the case of those in danger of death and as a preparation for certain duties requiring purity.

William of Occam (d. about 1349), many of whose ideas were taken over by Luther, carried this evolutionary process in the theology of penance to lengths that were condemned as heretical. For him, there is no question of attrition being necessary—much less of its being sufficient—to win God's forgiveness. God pardons sin without requiring any movement of repentance. According to this view, absolution merely *demonstrates* that the sinner *is* forgiven. Absolution does not loose; it supposes the remission of sins to be already accomplished. Absolution, then, is alone essential; contrition, confession, satisfaction are but conditions presupposed either in fact or in the desire or will. The sacrament, however, is necessary—at least it has to be desired (*in voto*)—for the remission of sins really to take place. This is pure nominalism, which empties the sacrament of all objective efficacy, locating in the intention, the desire, or the will (*in voto*) the whole essence of the spiritual life.

Thus in the Middle Ages, before the Reformation, certain questions were already being raised concerning the traditional

[1] On Duns Scotus and William of Occam, see *Dict. Théol. cath.*, Vol. XII, Col. 1027-41.

Catholic view of the sacrament of penance as it had been formulated by St Thomas.

In the Reformers, Luther and Calvin, we find the same difficulties, the same questions and the same replies as have been made from time to time throughout the history of Christianity in regard to the problem of confession.

Whereas Luther maintains the sacramental value of absolution, Calvin puts forward weighty objections against it. In *De captivitate Babylonica*[1] Luther asserts explicitly that he accepts three sacraments: Baptism, Penance, and the Bread. Nevertheless he does evince a certain hesitation on account of the lack of a divinely instituted sign. So Penance becomes a return to Baptism.[2] Melanchthon was to retain absolution as a third sacrament: 'If we call sacraments those rites which are ordained of God and to which the promise of grace has been added . . . then these are sacraments: Baptism, the Lord's Supper, and Absolution, which is the Sacrament of Penance.'[3] The Augsburg Confession declares: 'Repentance properly consists of these two parts,—one is contrition or a terror-stricken conscience on account of acknowledged sin; the other is faith, which is produced by the Gospel or by absolution, and believes that, for Christ's sake, sins are remitted, which tranquillizes the conscience and frees it from fear.'[4]

For Calvin, penance is not a sacrament, for 'it is not an external ceremony instituted by the Lord for the confirmation of our faith', and again because 'there is no promise of God, which is the only foundation of a Sacrament'; in fact, 'the promise of the keys does not pertain to the making of some particular state of absolution, but only to the preaching of the Gospel'.[5] It seems that if the

[1] *Luthers Werke*, Weimar Edition, Vol. VI, p. 501. See *Luther's Primary Works*, ed. Wace and Buchheim, Hodder & Stoughton, London, 1896, p. 294.
[2] *Luthers Werke*, p. 572. See *Luther's Primary Works*, p. 408.
[3] *Apologia confessionis*, art. 13 (7).
[4] Art. 12, *De paenitentia*. See W. H. Teale, *A Translation of the Confession of Augsburg*, T. W. Green, Leeds, 1842, Art. XII, 'Of Repentance', p. 40.
[5] *Institutes*, 1560 edition, Bk. IV, Ch. XIX, Paras. 15 and 17.

sacrament consisted in 'the absolution by the Priest' and not in the 'penitence, either internal or external',[1] Calvin would be disposed to understand it.[2] But he prefers not to make any concessions, and categorically to renounce Penance as a sacrament, even, it appears, in the Lutheran sense. His argument against Penance as a sacrament is limited to astonishment at the absence of a matter.

The absence of a 'matter' (as commonly understood) is not, however, a reason for there being no sacrament. The definition of a sacrament which he claims to take from St Augustine is one definition among many, arbitrary and extra-biblical. Furthermore, how is it that he does not see here the quite explicit promise made by Christ to his Apostles concerning the remission of sins? In conclusion, Calvin says: 'We shall speak with the greatest propriety, therefore, if we call Baptism a Sacrament of Penance.'[3]

As regards the sacramental character of Penance, the problem of the absence of a 'matter' was raised for Calvin just as it was raised for the Scotists. Do not St Thomas himself and the Council of Florence speak of 'matter, as it were' (*quasi materia*)?[4] Obviously, unqualified uniformity is not to be found among all the rites which have traditionally come to be called sacraments. Calvin is here insisting on an exactitude that is far too logical and geometrical.

The Reformers' criticism in regard to the three acts of penance —contrition, confession, and satisfaction—is much easier to understand, from their standpoint of justification only by faith, through God's grace alone.

In Luther's eyes contrition is impossible, and attrition is but an hypocritical caricature of it. Since man is basically sinful, he

---

[1] *Institutes, ibid.*, Para. 16.

[2] Although he is not here explicit on the point, Calvin, while seeing the value of Penance in 'the absolution by the Priest' rather than in the act of the penitent, is afraid that the pastoral ministry will be viewed as a magical priesthood if he attributes to Penance the value of a sacrament. We shall see later that Calvin, although eschewing the word in order to avoid the possibility of error, did not reject the sacramental reality of absolution. The point is an important one. In the same way we shall accept fully his criticism of the magical priesthood in the chapter on 'The Confessor'.

[3] *Institutes, ibid.*, Para. 17. [4] See notes 1 and 2, p. 63.

cannot be truly contrite; contrition therefore cannot validly form part of the Sacrament of Penance.

'The contrition which is prepared by the discussion, assembly, and detestation of the sins, by means of which a person goes over his life, in the bitterness of his soul, weighing the gravity, the multitude, and the vileness of his sins, the loss of eternal beatitude and the acquisition of eternal damnation, this contrition is hypocritical and makes the person an even greater sinner.'[1]

This extreme position of the early Luther must be viewed in the light of the controversy over the traffic in indulgences and absolution. The Reformer is particularly apprehensive of man putting his trust in anything but God's grace alone, known only by faith in Jesus Christ. 'Have no confidence in being absolved because of thy contrition, but because of Christ's words: "Whatsoever ye shall bind, etc." Put thy confidence in that thou shalt have received the absolution of the priest, and believe firmly that thou art absolved, and thou shalt indeed be absolved.'[2]

What we have here is the old problem of faith and works, which runs through all Luther's writings. The sacrament of penance consists essentially in the free action of God, faithful to his promise in Jesus Christ, which must be effective whatever the state of mind of the penitent. This extreme faith which Luther had in the efficacy of the sacrament in the believer is paradoxically expressed by him thus: 'If *per impossibile* the confessed person were in no degree contrite, or if the priest had given him absolution irresponsibly and lightly, yet if he believes himself to be absolved, he is in very truth absolved.'[3] This is not to say that sacramental efficacy depends only on faith. On the contrary, it depends on no human attitude or proceeding—neither on the sincerity of the contrition, nor on the completeness of the confession,[4] much less on satisfaction, however strictly accomplished—but on the promise of God alone, received by supernatural faith. If, however, there is

---

[1] *Sermo de paenitentia*, 1518, *Luthers Werke*, Vol. I, p. 319.
[2] *Ibid.*, p. 323.   [3] *Ibid.*, p. 323.
[4] 'It is impossible to know all one's mortal sins', *ibid.*, p. 322.

no faith at all, then the sacrament is of no effect: 'No man's sins are remitted if he does not believe they are remitted, when the priest remits them.'[1]

There is no absolute obligation to practise confession, for Luther, but he does not exclude pressing exhortation within the Church to a regular discipline of confession. In 1529 he added to the second edition of the *Great Catechism* a 'Short exhortation to Confession'.[2] At the beginning he writes: 'Concerning confession, we have always taught that it must be free.'[3] Then, having distinguished between confession to God alone and that made to one's neighbour in order to redress an injury, he goes on: 'There is private confession, which is made to one brother. . . . Private confession is not rendered obligatory by any commandment. . . . Each is free to use it when he feels the need of it.'[4] Private confession is composed of two parts: our own act and the act of God. On the one hand 'we groan under the weight of our sins and we ask for consolation and comfort for our souls'; on the other hand, God, 'by the word which he has placed in the mouth of man, absolves me from my sins'. Here Luther is less categorical regarding the action of the penitent—contrition. Ten years have passed; the controversy over indulgences has lost much of its importance; experience of pastoral ministry has brought him back to a more balanced view of Christ's Gospel. Nevertheless he maintains that 'we must consider our action as of little account, and, conversely, we must attach the greatest importance to the Word of God'. We must go to confession in order to receive, not to give. Contrition does not consist in the recitation of a catalogue of sins, but 'what matters is that you should bewail your misery and seek help, in order to have once more a joyful heart and conscience'. It is better to abstain from confession than to go to it unwillingly or in order to do a good work. But Luther zealously urges the practice of

[1] *Resolutiones disputationum de indulgentiarum virtute*, 1518, Concl. 7; *Luthers Werke*, Vol. I, p. 543.
[2] *Les livres symboliques*, Editions Je Sers, Paris, 1947, pp. 227-33. See my Conclusion, p. 142.
[3] *Op. cit.*, p. 227.   [4] *Op. cit.*, p. 229.

private confession—'our dear confession', as he calls it. 'If a poor miserable beggar heard that in a certain place were being distributed rich alms of money and clothing, would he need to be taken there by a policeman? . . . If you are poor and in misery, go and confess, and use this means to health. . . . If, however, you despise this treasure, and *if you are too proud to confess your sins, we conclude that you are no Christian*, and that neither ought you to share in the Sacrament (of the Lord's Supper). You despise what no Christian ought to despise, and therefore *you cannot obtain remission of your sins*, and from that we see also that *you despise the Gospel.*' One can hardly imagine a more telling exhortation to sacramental confession. No law, no obligation, but instead the description of a treasure of consolation which attracts us, poor and in misery as we are. If we do not practise confession we are not truly Christians, says Luther. 'So when I urge the practice of confession, I am but urging every man to be a Christian.'[1] Luther, with the Church of Christ, realized that the Christian, although living in the liberty of grace, and no longer in subjection to a constraining law, must be helped in his liberty by a discipline which makes that liberty real and prevents its being corrupted. Luther will not allow to 'enjoy our liberty' those who, under pretext of following the Gospel more closely, dispense with all discipline, particularly that of confession. 'For those among the people who will not obey the Gospel, it is necessary that there be a gaoler, to be for them the devil and executioner of God.'[2] It is better to be 'compelled' to practise confession, to fast, etc. . . . 'than to despise the voluntary and joyous discipline of confession, fasting, etc. . . . Like as the hart desireth the water-brooks: so longeth my soul for the Word of God, for absolution and for the Sacrament'.[3]

For his part Calvin, while rejecting penance as a sacrament, nevertheless upholds non-obligatory private confession. It should be noted that his criticism of the sacrament of penance dates almost in its entirety from his first edition of the *Institutes of*

[1] *Op. cit.*, p. 233.   [2] *Op. cit.*, p. 228.   [3] *Op. cit.*, p. 233.

the Christian Religion (1536). In the editions of 1539 and 1541 some important changes have been made in his criticism. He maintains his refusal to recognize penance as a sacrament, still emphasizing that the power of the keys is to be understood only in the sense of 'the preaching of the Gospel'.[1] In his chapter on repentance in general, he develops also his exegesis of the Epistle of St James (5.16), showing that what is referred to there is mutual confession, a sort of sharing: 'That is to say that we should communicate and disclose our infirmities to each other, to receive advice, compassion, and mutual consolation.'[2] Nevertheless, and this must be seen—as with Luther—as the fruit of experience of pastoral ministry, he is much more positive regarding a certain sort of private confession. From 1538 to 1541 he was pastor at Strasbourg, under the influence of that nice theologian Bucer; the influence of the aged Luther made itself felt. In 1536 he had come to recognize, like Luther, three sorts of confession: to God alone, to a brother with a view to mutual aid by 'advice and consolation', to a brother against whom we have offended, 'recognizing our guilt and asking for forgiveness'.[3] In 1539 he added a very important paragraph. On the subject of the second kind of confession, which in 1536 he had considered only as mutual, on the basis of his interpretation of St James, he wrote: 'Though the Scripture, by not expressly appointing any one to whom we should disburden ourselves, leaves us at liberty to confess to any member of the Church who shall appear most suitable; yet, *since the Pastors must be considered more proper for this than others, we ought chiefly to make choice of them. I say that they are more suitable than others,* since, in their very vocation to the ministry, they are *designated by God, to instruct us to subdue our sins, and to certify us of God's goodness, for our consolation.* Therefore, let every believer, if he feels such perplexity of conscience that he cannot do without the help of another person, consider that he ought not to neglect the

---

[1] *Institution chrétienne*, Editions Belles-Lettres, Vol. IV, p. 88. He maintained this position in the edition of 1560, Bk. IV, Ch. XIX, Para. 17.
[2] *Op. cit.*, Vol. II, p. 194.   [3] *Ibid.*, pp. 199-200.

remedy offered him by God: which is, that in order to alleviate his distress and deliver himself from scruple, *he should confess privately to his pastor, and receive consolation from him*, whose office it is, both privately and publicly, to comfort the people of God with the doctrine of the Gospel. Nevertheless we must always so act that *men's consciences be not bound* and subjected to any yoke, where God has left us free to choose.'[1]

This passage asserts most clearly the usefulness of *private confession*, that *pastors* are the *ministers of absolution* ('to certify us of God's goodness, for our consolation'), and true *spiritual directors* ('to instruct us to subdue our sins'). Calvin clearly upholds the freedom of this most useful confession: '. . . that men's consciences be not bound.' He recognizes that the practice of confession is extremely ancient. 'But we can easily prove that at first it was free.'[2] Calvin had read Sozomen's account of the suppression by Nectarius (Bishop of Constantinople from 381 to 397) of the office of penitentiary priest and of private confession in Constantinople as a result of a certain scandal.[3] He had also read

---

[1] *Op. cit.*, Vol. II, p. 200.   [2] *Ibid.*, p. 195.
[3] Sozomenus, 'Ecclesiastical History', VII, 16, in *A Select Library of Nicene and Post-Nicene Fathers of the Christian Church*, Second Series, edited by H. Wace and P. Schaff, Parke and Co., Oxford, 1891, p. 386. Calvin believes with Sozomen that the scandal consisted in the fact that a certain lady of Constantinople, under colour of confession, had sexual relations with a deacon. But Socrates Scholasticus, the first narrator of the affair (see his 'Ecclesiastical History', V, XIX, *loc. cit.*, p. 128) relates that the lady had not been a penitent of the deacon, but that after she had confessed the liaison to a penitentiary priest, it had come about that the deacon had been deposed and that the affair had been ventilated in public. The resulting scandal had brought about the suppression of the penitentiaries. The scandal had been due not to the relations between confessor and penitent (as Calvin avers, repeating Sozomen's view); rather had it been created because a disciplinary measure had been taken on the basis of a confession, and because the penitentiary had not preserved the secrecy of confession, this last, as we shall see later, being a discipline essential to the practice of private confession.
In any case the results of the suppression of private confession at Constantinople were not good, for Socrates adds at the end of his account: 'My observation to Eudaemon' (the priest who had recommended the suppression to Nectarius) 'when he first related the circumstance was this: "Whether, O presbyter, your counsel has been profitable to the Church or otherwise, God knows; but I see that it takes away the means

St John Chrysostom, whom he quotes abundantly in support of the freedom of confession. It is not however certain that he understood him correctly, for the latter's purpose was to free believers from the necessity of public confession ('before witness') and not from private confession, which was little practised in his day and disparaged by those who admitted repentance only once, after baptism. Socrates also passes severe judgement on St John Chrysostom who, as he records, 'did not scruple to say: "Approach, although you may have repented a thousand times." For this doctrine, many even of his friends censured him.'[1] The Synod of the Oak had also reproved the saintly archbishop for his leniency. Bishop Isaac quotes him as saying: 'If you have sinned a second time, repent a second time; every time you sin, come to me and I shall heal you.'[2] Thus St John Chrysostom did not oppose auricular confession in favour of confession to God alone, as Calvin thought, but rather maintained, against the rigorists, the possibility of an infinite and inexhaustible divine mercy, operating when penitence is repeated again and again. It was his wish to liberate believers from the harsh demands made upon them by the single public repentance after baptism, by giving them the possibility of a number of repentances made before God. The problem facing the Archbishop of Constantinople was not the same as that with which the Reformer had to deal. Calvin went constantly for support to the tradition of the Early Fathers, but was sometimes too quick to take advantage of a text which sounded well to his own ears, as if their problems were the same as his.

The 1560 edition of the *Institutes* shows a marked development in Calvin's thought, certainly due once more to the influence of Strasbourg and to his pastoral experience. In the passage I have

of rebuking one another's faults, and prevents our acting upon the precept of the apostle: Have no fellowship with the unfruitful works of darkness, but rather reprove them".'

[1] 'Ecclesiastical History', VI, XXI.

[2] Mansi, *Sacrorum Conciliorum nova et amplissima collectio*, Arnhem and Leipzig, 1759-1927, Vol. III, Col. 1145 D.

quoted from the 1539 edition, where he says that the pastors are 'designated by God, to instruct us to subdue our sins, and to certify us of God's goodness, for our consolation', he inserted, in 1545, the following very important development: 'For though the office of mutual admonition is committed to all Christians, yet it is especially confided to ministers. And so, while we all ought mutually to console each other, yet we see that *ministers are constituted by God witnesses and as it were sureties, to certify our consciences of the remission of sins; insomuch that they themselves are said to remit sins and loose souls* (Matt. 16.19; 18.18; John 20.23). *When we find this attributed to them, let us consider that it is for our benefit.*'[1]

This is a long way from the superficial exegesis of James 5.16 or of Christ's words concerning the power of the keys. Calvin still insists on the fact that pastors are in a very special way the ministers of confession, 'constituted by God witnesses and as it were sureties, to certify our consciences of the remission of sins'. Pastors are not only witnesses proclaiming the remission of sins, their function is not only to preach the Gospel; they are as it were sureties for the remission of sins. For that is in fact what Calvin means by the word *pleige*, which he uses here and also, for example, in the chapter of the *Institutes* dealing with 'The difference of the two Testaments'.[2]

Echoing the words of the Epistle to the Hebrews (7.22), he speaks of Jesus Christ as 'surety (*pleige*) and Mediator of a better covenant'. He uses the French word *pleige* to translate the Latin word *sponsor*, which means surety, bailman, guarantor (of someone's promises).[3] It is interesting to note that Calvin uses the word

[1] *Institutes*, 1560 edition, Bk. III, Ch. IV, Para. 12. See my introduction, p. 19. This text dates from 1545.

[2] *Op. cit.*, Bk. II, Ch. XI, Para. 4.

[3] The same meaning is given to the word *pleige* when Calvin adds it in 1541 as an explanation of the word 'ransom' in paragraph 30 of the same chapter on penitence (Bk. III, Ch. IV, in the edition of 1560). 'Christ gave himself a ransom for us: that is to say that he made himself a surety (*pleige*) in our stead in order to deliver us fully from all the debts of our sins.'

in connection with the Epistle to the Hebrews to signify the ministry of Christ, and in the context with which we are dealing to designate the role of the pastor in the exercise of his ministry as a confessor. The pastor is joined to Christ the High Priest in the exercise of this solemn office. His ministry is the present manifestation of the eternal mediation of Christ. Christ is surety or guarantor; the pastor is as it were (*quasi*) surety or guarantor; his ministry is dependent upon the priesthood of Jesus Christ: it shows it forth. This word *quasi* postulates a special relationship between the one and only guarantor of the remission of sins, and all pastors as guarantors of the promises of Jesus Christ. One may discern here the traditional conception, which goes back to the Epistle to the Hebrews, of the ministry of the Church and of the pastor as a sacramental priesthood, as a priesthood which signifies, manifests, shows forth and actualizes the unique and eternal priesthood of the one Mediator, Jesus Christ, which he himself exercises in the Church.

Thus it is the duty of pastors, when the conscience of the believer is overburdened, to vouch for the promises of God in Jesus Christ; they stand surety for those promises, guarantee them as it were, when they loose souls by the good news of the Gospel in absolution. To such an extent are they the guarantors of the mercy of God 'that they themselves,' adds Calvin, 'are said to remit sins and loose souls'. There can be no doubt that Calvin is here interpreting the words of Jesus to the Apostles after his resurrection (John 20.23), and the power of the keys (Matt. 16.19; 18.18), in the traditional sense of the sacrament of absolution: the Church, by the word of its ministers founded on the promise of Jesus Christ, has power to remit sins and loose souls. But we must beware of making too much of Calvin's words. It is necessary to say at once that the whole context of his thoughts on penitence and the power of the keys shows that he attributes this power of absolution not to the Church or the minister in themselves, but in so far as they preach the Gospel. Has the authentic Christian tradition ever thought otherwise, divided the ministry of Christ and that of the priest, except in periods of theological poverty, such as, in fact, the period of late Scholasticism in the fifteenth and sixteenth centuries?

It is then as a healthy reaction after a period of deviation that Calvin here rejoins the authentic tradition of the Early Fathers: the minister is constituted by God a witness and guarantor to certify consciences of the remission of sins by the Gospel of which his word is the bearer, so that one may say that he remits sins and looses souls. What we have here is the traditional sacrament of absolution, although Calvin denies elsewhere that he recognizes any sacramental value in penance. The theology of his time does not permit him to indulge in a rational line of thought. He must be a purist in opposition to a decadent sacramental theology.

While he stresses their close relationship, Calvin does not make absolution merely a form of preaching. He considers it truly to be *a confirmation and a seal*[1] of the grace of the Gospel. The apparent contradictions in his thought derive from his fear of sacramental superstition and magic from which he wishes to protect Christian people. We too must eschew it. The safest way is always to maintain, like Calvin, the relationship between Word and Sacrament, between Scripture, read and preached, the letter of God, and the sacramental Sign, the signature or seal affixed by God, to '*seal* in our consciences the promises of his good-will towards us, to *confirm* [=strengthen] the weakness of our faith'.[2] As far as the sacrament of absolution is concerned, this means that if we are led to distinguish it from the cure of souls or spiritual direction, we must not divorce it from them entirely by neglecting them. To do so would be to fall back into a magical, automatic view of confession. Absolution must be followed by spiritual direction,

[1] It is well known that Calvin constantly employs the image of the seal to designate the sacrament which seals the Word in us. 'Nor can it be objected [by those who deny the value of the sacrament] that this similitude has been recently invented by us; for it has been used by St Paul, who calls the Sacrament of Circumcision a seal: σφραγῖδα.' (*Institutes*, 1560 edition, Bk. IV, Ch. XIV, Para. 5.)

[2] *Ibid.*, Para. 1.

by counsel founded on the Word of God, if not immediately (as we shall see), at least in connection with the confession. Thus for us Sacrament and Word will be inseparably bound up together, in accordance with Calvin's salutary warning. This said, we must emphasize the sacramental character which the Reformer undoubtedly attributes to absolution in pastoral, if not in dogmatic theology. On the one hand he is able to declare in 1536, and repeat in 1560: 'I deny that it [the act of penitence as a whole: contrition, confession, absolution, and satisfaction] ought to be considered as a Sacrament.'[1] And on the other he adds in 1560: 'Its whole force and meaning consists in this, that the grace of the Gospel should be *confirmed* and *sealed*, as it were, in public as well as in private, by those whom God has ordained to this office; which cannot be done but by preaching alone.'[2] And a few pages further on he writes: 'Absolution is conditional, in such a way, that the sinner may be confident that God is propitious to him, provided he sincerely seeks an atonement in the sacrifice of Christ, and relies upon the grace offered to him. Thus *it is impossible for the pastor to err*, who according to his office promulgates what he has been taught *by the word of God*: and the sinner for his part receives *a quite certain and clear absolution*, simply on condition of *embracing the grace of Christ*, according to the general rule of our good Lord . . .—"According to your faith be it done unto you" (Matt. 9.29).'[3]

Absolution is conditional: faith is necessary for it to be effectively received. It must be taken as a sign of grace, like the Lord's Supper, for it to act effectively. But then its action is *infallible*, it is quite certain and clear. Calvin teaches that a sacrament does not act like a magic spell, but that it is an effective sign. It must be understood as a sign by the faith of the believer enlightened by the Word of God, and thus taken it acts effectively and infallibly. The sacraments, illuminated by the Word, are a source of absolute peace, confidence, and assurance.

[1] *Institutes*, 1560 edition, Bk. IV, Ch. XIX, Para. 17.
[2] *Op. cit.*, Bk. III, Ch. IV, Para. 14.   [3] *Ibid.*, Para. 22.

This is the Calvinistic and Patristic doctrine of the *effective sign*. The biblical text here referred to by Calvin (Matt. 9.29) leads to the same conclusions. He quotes the healing by Jesus of the two blind men in order to illustrate the role of faith in absolution. The account of this miracle is very apt for an understanding of what happens in the sacrament of absolution. The two blind men cry after Jesus: 'Thou son of David, have mercy on us.' It is a confession of sin and of human misery. Jesus puts to them the question of faith, the condition of the miracle: 'Believe ye that I am able to do this?' It is not enough to desire the miracle, healing, or forgiveness; it is necessary to believe in it. They reply: 'Yea, Lord.' Then, in response to their faith, Christ touches their eyes and says: 'According to your faith be it unto you.' And their eyes were opened. 'According to your faith' does not mean 'in the measure of your faith', but 'because you believe'. Indeed, how could our faith, tinier than a grain of mustard-seed, ever be set in the balance against God's miraculous action or his forgiveness? It is enough that our faith be like a little grain for mountains to be removed. It is enough to believe quite humbly and simply in the infinite mercy of the Lord, for our eyes to be opened by the imposition of his hands, and our sin remitted.

'When we find this attributed to pastors, let us consider that it is for our benefit,' Calvin concludes. God has indeed attributed to pastors this sacramental ministry of absolution, and it is very beneficial to us.

Calvin goes on to state his views on the freedom of confession. As in 1539, he says that 'we should always be careful to lay no yoke on the conscience, where God has given no positive command'. But then he adds: 'Hence it follows that such confession ought to be free, so as not to be exacted of any, but only *to be recommended as a useful aid to those who need it.*' To the assertion of the freedom of confession Calvin feels it necessary to add the need of an exhortation to practise it as a 'useful aid'.

A little further on he urges once more the benefits of confession: 'For it sometimes happens, that he who hears the general promises of God, which are addressed to the whole Church, nevertheless remains in some suspense, and is still *disquieted with doubts as to the forgiveness of his sins*. But *if he discloses secretly to his Pastor his distress*, and hears the Pastor applying to him *in particular* the general doctrine, he will be *straightly assured* where formerly he was in doubt, and will be *liberated* from every trepidation and find repose of conscience.'[1]

When Calvin wrote: 'It is not therefore to be wondered at that we reject this auricular confession, as being a pestilential thing and in so many ways pernicious for the Church,' he could only have had in mind a distortion of the true tradition of confession. In fact in 1560 it is none other than this true private confession which is described to us. Does he not speak of '*disclosing secretly* one's distress' to the Pastor, who is then to 'apply in particular the general doctrine'? What is that but private confession as the authentic tradition of the Church has always understood it?[2]

We can therefore sum up the Reformers' final position with regard to the sacrament of penance as defined by Scholasticism and as practised at that time in the Roman Church: the act of 'penance' consists rather in the *absolution* than in the contrition, confession and satisfaction, rather in the *promise* of God and the *faith* of the penitent than in works of reparation. Such works are the signs of mercy freely granted, and never a condition of forgiveness. Absolution is *sacramental* for the Lutherans; it is linked with the *particular preaching* of the Gospel for the Calvinists. *Contrition* is always imperfect and is only a more or less 'hypocritical' sign of our sinful nature, although necessary. *Confession* is useful but must remain free. There is no *satisfaction* possible ('by prayer, fasting, and almsgiving'), Christ alone having made satisfaction, once for all; nevertheless it is necessary to make amends for one's sins to those one has wronged.[3] The usual

---

[1] *Op. cit.*, Bk. III, Ch. IV, Para. 14.

[2] On Calvin and the cure of souls see J. D. Benoit, *Calvin, directeur d'âmes*, Oberlin, Strasbourg, 1947.

[3] Quoting Hosea 14.1-2, Calvin writes concerning satisfaction: 'There [in the sacrifice of our lips] is satisfaction, which is but thanksgiving.'

minister of confession is the pastor. The effect of 'penitence' is the *remission of sins*, and *renewed obedience*. In Scholastic form the Confession of Erlau (1562) thus sums up the Reformed doctrine of penitence: 'The efficient cause of penitence is the grace of God; the merit of penitence is Christ; the formal cause is the Holy Ghost; the instrumental cause is faith together with the word (absolution, Gospel); the final cause is renewed obedience.'[1]

And elsewhere: ' "Thy faith," Jesus said to the woman who was a sinner, "hath saved thee." It is, then, by faith that we obtain remission: and by *charity we render thanks* and acknowledge the liberality of our Lord' (*Institutes*, Bk. III, Ch. IV, Paras. 30 and 37).

[1] E. F. K. Müller, *Die Bekenntnisschriften der reformierten Kirchen*, Leipzig, 1903, p. 289.

CHAPTER TWO

COMMUNION IN SIN AND ECCLESIASTICAL DISCIPLINE

THE Church, which is the Body of Christ, realizes among its various members not only a community of faith and spiritual life, but also a communion in suffering and sin. Pain suffered by one member affects the whole organism; the impurity of one member contaminates the whole body. 'Whether one member suffer', writes St Paul, 'all the members suffer with it' (I Cor. 12.26). The first Epistle to the Corinthians goes a long way in its affirmation of the reality of communion in evil (both suffering and sin).

The Corinthian Christians are tolerating an incestuous person among their number. The Apostle warns them of the danger of this by comparing the sin of one individual with a little leaven that 'leaveneth the whole lump' (I Cor. 5.6-8). Leaven, in Jewish tradition, was a symbol of impurity—the Passover was to be celebrated with unleavened bread. St Paul uses this image in order to exhort the Christians of Corinth to beware of the contagion of sin in the Church, 'old leaven . . . the leaven of malice and wickedness'. The leaven may contaminate the whole loaf, making it rise. The image is a double one: as the leaven contaminates and causes the dough to rise, so the sin of one defiles and sets in revolt against God the whole Church, so closely are its members bound together. The Church must become a 'new lump' by ridding itself of all the leaven of impurity, malice, and wickedness, so that it may keep the perpetual feast of the Passover of Christ 'with the unleavened bread of sincerity and truth'. If the Church does not live in this sincerity and truth, if it tolerates in its bosom impurity and falsehood, it is not what it must always be becoming afresh: a new lump. 'Transparency' is thus seen to be a necessity of nature and of existence for the Church. If the members of the Church do not live in that transparency of life which is purity and sincerity, truth and loyalty, the Church is polluted. She must be on the watch, therefore, to purge herself of all the leaven of malice and wickedness, in order to rediscover purity and truth, the quality of a new lump, which it is her true nature to be and which she must always be becoming. Christ who has been sacrificed is indeed our Passover, that is to say the pure, sincere, true, and loyal unleavened bread which the Church must be. There can be no true communion with Christ without that sincerity and truth. 'Blessed are the pure in heart: for they shall see God' (Matt. 5.8).

This communion in sin, this contagion in impurity and falsehood, requires of the Church discipline and keen vigilance. Certain associations must be broken off in order to safeguard purity and truth, in order to retain the communion with the Lord. 'Ye cannot drink the cup of the Lord, and the cup of devils' (I Cor. 10.21). The Christian is to have no company with fornicators, the covetous, idolaters, revilers, drunkards, extortioners . . . (I Cor. 5.9-10). 'If any man obey not our word by this epistle, note that man, and have no company with him,' writes St Paul to the Thessalonians (II Thess. 3.14). St Paul does not mean the generality of fornicators, or the covetous, or extortioners, or idolaters of this world, 'for then ye must needs go out of this world' (I Cor. 5.10). All puritanism or moralism is thus excluded. The Christian must be in the world without being of the world. He must not even 'judge them that are without'. He must be full of understanding, indulgence, and compassion towards those who do not know Christ. It is God alone who judges them and knows their lot. It is 'them that are within' whom we are to judge (I Cor. 5.12). The Church must show a certain severity in her love towards any of her members who live in impurity and falsehood, who persist in their sin in despite of the Christian life. This severity may seem harsh to Christians today, accustomed to facile, indulgent, and irresponsible charity. St Paul speaks of not eating with anyone like the incestuous man of Corinth, or any other such sinner in the Church. The meal is here the chief sign of brotherly communion. To eat with a person is to know that one has a quite special relationship with him. The meal is for our relationship with men what the Lord's Supper is for our communion with the Body of Christ. St Paul, conscious of the deep significance of the shared meal, and especially the meal shared by Christians, urges the faithful to banish from their table any Christian who is a notorious sinner. Why this severity in a Church which believes in the infinite mercy of God and the boundless love of Jesus Christ? Are we not to forgive 'until seventy times seven' (Matt. 18.21-2)? How is it possible to judge a brother, when Christ himself exhorts us not to behold the mote which is in our brother's eye, but to consider the beam that is in our own (Matt. 7.3-5)? Is not the door open to hypocrisy? 'Thou hypocrite, first cast out the beam out of thine own eye; and then shalt thou see clearly to cast out the mote out of thy brother's eye.'

This judgement is not an individual judgement, but a discipline exercised by the community, by the Church. The individual has no right to judge; he must judge only himself, and in humility consider others as superior to himself. In fact his own sins must always be for him like a beam in comparison with the sin of others, which he must think of as like a mote. It is a spiritual judgement made in humility, which takes no account of the objective importance of the sin. Only the Church as such can pass judgement on a man's sin and exercise a discipline which excludes the sinner from the community in order to receive him back afterwards.

This is how St Matthew describes the Church's discipline (Matt. 18.15-22). The first recourse of a Christian in regard to a brother who has sinned, is fraternal exhortation in private. If the sinner pays heed, he is won over, pardoned, liberated. If he does not listen, he must be exhorted with one or two witnesses. The matter has become more serious, in fact. There are signs of hardening in the sinner, and in order to overcome the power of evil in him the more effective words of two or three witnesses are required. There is no question here, of course, of private, personal sin, but of public or scandalous wrongdoing already known to several people. Intimate sin cannot be the object of this sort of discipline, since in such a case the exercise of confession implies absolute secrecy. But I quote this example of ecclesiastical discipline simply because I believe all sin, of whatever kind, to have repercussions on the level of the community, affecting the whole Church. If in private confession this ecclesiastical discipline cannot be exercised out of respect for the secrecy of the confessional and in order to avoid disturbance and scandal among weaker brethren, this does not mean that the confessor ought not to consider himself as exercising the ministry of the Church herself as he listens and pardons; and in the same way the person who is confessing must be conscious of admitting his sin before a man who represents for him the whole company of the Church.

Sin, whether private or public, can never be looked upon as a mere personal shortcoming. Not only does even the most secret sin create an attitude which disturbs the peace and the joy of the community, not only has it psychological consequences which shed abroad some degree of disorder and suffering; any sin, however secret, since it is the sin of a member of the body, is a drag on the Church because it causes a rupture in her relationship with God. If we were less individualistic in our faith and in our repentance, we should have a profounder realization of the unhappy consequences of our sin, as well as being freer and more whole-hearted in our struggle against the Devil. That, after all, is how we ought to consider the exercise of ecclesiastical discipline on the one hand, and the practice of confession on the other—as a battle against Satan. It is most certainly not a case of analysing a psychological and spiritual situation and lamenting our incapacities or our complexes. A quite objective battle is being fought within us, one of the factors making for victory being confession followed by absolution. Neither in the exercise of ecclesiastical discipline nor in the practice of private confession are we called upon to sit in judgement over an individual, overwhelming him with a sense of the enormity of his faults. What is required rather is to associate the Church or a confessor in the struggle which the sinner must carry on against Satan. To associate the sinner in the objective struggle of the Church against the powers of evil is not to lessen his individual responsibility or blame; but instead of turning the perplexities of sin into a despairing struggle against oneself, confession makes possible for the Church and for the believer the hope of victory over the Devil through a battle nobly fought. 'Be strong in the Lord, and in the power of his might. Put on the whole armour of God, that ye may be able to stand against the wiles of the devil. For we wrestle not against flesh and blood, but against principalities, against powers, against the rulers of the darkness of this world, against spiritual wickedness in high places' (Eph. 6.10-12). The exercise of ecclesiastical discipline and private confession, then, are the waging of this grand campaign against all the forces of the evil one. They provide the sinner with powerful arms for the fight. This is not a battle against flesh and blood—it is not, that is, a matter of humiliating the sinner by treating him as having inherited evil tendencies, as being sick, 'complex-ridden', or neurotic; rather is it a battle against enemies without and within, a good warfare into which he may enter filled with a high hope of victory.

This idea of a battle against the powers of evil, fought by the Church with the sinner, is brought out by several passages in the New Testament dealing with excommunication. Although these texts have nothing to do with private confession, in which there can be no question of the exercise of any external discipline, they are worth studying in order that we may be convinced that the Church's fight against sin does not imply an humiliating judgement upon the sinner, or a severity that excludes him from the fellowship of the faithful. The opposite is the case: they will show us that when the Church exercises her discipline, it is her way of loving better. After all, would the Church be loving if she shut her eyes to the disorder, error, and sin which may turn men away from Jesus Christ? The love, the charity which goes beyond mere human affection, often weak and indulgent as the latter is, calls for truth, sincerity, and purity in a way which may sometimes seem severe, but which leads in the end to a greater love, since it allows the sinner to remain or to return within the fellowship of Christ. Though the love of the Church is patient and kind, it cannot rejoice at injustice, or wink at it; but it rejoices in the truth. Love 'beareth all things': that is not to say that it closes its eyes to sin, but that it knows who is the author and what is the source of all sin. The forbearance of love does not do away with the responsibility of the sinner, but it restores him to the order of battle of the whole Christian community against the forces of evil, not as a renegade, but as a warrior equipped with the armour of God. Love 'believeth all things': that is not to say that truth is a matter of indifference to it, but that it trusts the sincerity of the confession of the man who is a sinner. Love 'hopeth all things': which is to say that it reckons no sin to be an inheritance of the flesh and the blood, like some incurable disease; but it knows that victory is certain and that Christ has won it already. Love 'endureth all things': that is to say that it is not astonished or frightened by sin, but is willing to share all the burdens that his sinful human nature lays on the shoulders of every man.

St Paul, in exhorting the Thessalonians to have no dealings with any man who does not obey the commands contained in his letter, is not being purely negative in his judgement or in the course he advises. Such a discipline of exclusion must make the sinner ashamed, not in order to crush him with a subjective sense of guilt, but to bring him to the victory of Christ over Satan in him. Indeed, the Apostle adds: 'Yet count him not as an enemy, but admonish him as a brother' (II Thess. 3.15). The sinner still remains in the Church, a brother. Even when discipline requires the temporary exclusion of a notorious sinner from the Eucharistic fellowship, he remains the object of the Church's maternal care. He may be considered as a heathen and a publican (Matt. 18.17), but this can only mean that he becomes once more one of those to whom the Church has a quite special duty of preaching the Gospel, in whom she must fight the battle against Satan. Was not Jesus called the friend of publicans and sinners (Matt. 11.19)? If therefore the Church looks upon the notorious sinner as a heathen and a publican, it is in order to have once more with him that original relationship of Christ with sinners. When St Paul declares that he has delivered to Satan Hymenaeus and Alexander, it is, he says, 'that they may learn not to blaspheme' (I Tim. 1.20). To deliver them to Satan is to put them for a time outside the communion of the Church, that is to say into the realm of the princes of this world of darkness, so that, deprived of the special means of grace of the community, and particularly of the Lord's Supper, they may realize the consequences of the error of their ways. This is a positive judgement whose purpose is to bring them back to a proper conception of the Resurrection, and a better conscience (I Tim. 1.19; II Tim. 2.18). The same is to apply to the incestuous man of Corinth. Although absent in body St Paul is in union with the Church, and by the power of Jesus Christ has pronounced his judgement: 'In the name of our Lord Jesus Christ . . . to deliver such an one unto Satan for the destruction of the flesh, that the spirit may be saved in the day of the Lord Jesus' (I Cor. 5.4-5). We have here a primitive formula of excommunication. The Church, through its apostolic ministry, wields the power of judgement which is the Lord's. Here again the delivery to Satan is for the destruction of the flesh, that is to say, for the annihilation of the demoniac powers and the sinful self that has handed itself over to them. Here the flesh signifies, not the flesh and blood of our inherited humanity, but everything in us which is in thrall to the power of sin because of our passionate and perverse propensities. It is for our salvation at the last day that that flesh must be destroyed.

The sentence of excommunication, therefore, is a sign of mercy rather than of condemnation. To shut the eyes to sin, to the sinner and to scandal, would be a lack of true love and a failure to care about man's salvation, since it would mean denying him the conditions and the opportunity for true repentance and re-conversion. The ancient discipline of the Church allowed penitents to wage the good warfare of Christ against the Devil in the exorcisms of Lent. The daily liturgy allowed them to re-learn the great truths of the Gospel, and its prayers to express their repentance and their expectancy of forgiveness. The Feast of Easter crowned this warfare with their reintegration into the Eucharistic communion with their risen Lord. The monotony and toughness of our Christian lives sometimes makes us wish that we also had this opportunity of fighting effectively against Satan in the liturgical communion of the Church.

The participation of the whole company of the faithful, in humility and penitence, in the 'exorcism' of the sin and the reconciliation of the sinner, is clearly revealed in the acts of public penance practised in the early Church. The bishop himself, who pronounces absolution, humbles himself on account of the sin for which all—and he first—are responsible, and in prayer engages in an objective battle against the Devil, a battle which the penitent will continue in his own home. This solidarity in sin, without any condemnation of the sinner, and this collective imploring of forgiveness, like the battle against Satan, are the characteristic signs of a Church with a real community life, in which confession can be effectively practised. The following account is an illustration of it.

Sozomenus relates how the reconciliation of penitents was carried out in Rome in the fourth century: 'At Rome . . . there is a place appropriated to the reception of penitents, in which spot they stand and mourn until the completion of the services, for it is not lawful for them to take part in the mysteries; then they cast themselves with groans and lamentations, prostrate on the ground. The bishop conducts the ceremony, sheds tears, and prostrates himself in like manner; and all the people burst into tears, and groan aloud. Afterwards, the bishop rises first from the ground, and raises up the others; he offers up prayer on behalf of the penitents, and then dismisses them. Each of the penitents subjects himself in private to voluntary suffering, either by fastings, by abstaining from the bath or from divers kinds of meats, or by other prescribed means, until a certain period appointed by the bishop. When the time arrives, he is made free from the consequences of his sin, and assembles at the church with the people. The Roman priests have carefully observed this custom from the beginning to the present time.'[1]

[1] *Op. cit.*, p. 386.

CHAPTER THREE

THE POWER TO FORGIVE

PRIMITIVE religious art often represented the sacramental acts of the Church in the form of an incident from the Bible. Beside representations of Baptism and the Lord's Supper one often sees, as the third panel of a triptych, an illustration of Absolution. In the Roman catacombs the picture of the healing of the paralytic is used to illustrate this side of the Church's ministry. The primitive community saw in this story the institution and the revelation of the power to forgive. In answer to the outraged intervention of certain scribes, Jesus orders the paralytic to stand up. 'For whether is easier, to say, Thy sins be forgiven thee; or to say, Arise and walk? But that ye may know that the Son of man hath power on earth to forgive sins (then saith he to the sick of the palsy), Arise, take up thy bed and go unto thine house' (Matt. 9.5-6). One can understand how shocked the Jews were to hear a man arrogate to himself the right to forgive sins. Their theology aimed at safe-guarding at all costs the transcendence of God and his rights. To forgive sins is to make use of a power which belongs to God alone. How can an ordinary man have the right to loose his neighbour from the bonds of guilt? Absolution can only be preached; then by faith the sinner appropriates the preaching to himself, and so there is implanted in him the certainty of God's forgiveness. This conception sometimes reappears in Protestantism. It would seem that belief in the transcendence of God excludes the possi-bility of the Church declaring the forgiveness of sins and really giving absolution. The Incarnation has put this Judaistic concep-tion out of date. The Son of Man really has power on earth to forgive sins. In his humanity, Christ can absolve, and as a sign of this, he heals the paralytic. 'When the multitude saw it, they marvelled and glorified God, which had given such power unto men' (Matt. 9.8). The power to forgive, like that of healing, since it is the privilege of the Son of Man, is also 'given unto men' in so far as they are united with Christ in the Church. The Church, the Body of Christ, which means today the humanity of Jesus at work in this world, retains this power of absolution. It is not a question only of preaching forgiveness, but of actually granting it. The Church has not only a duty to preach the divine mercy in order to arouse faith and the assurance of forgiveness, but also the power effectively to remit sins by the efficacious sign of absolution.

This ministry of absolution forms part of the mission of the Apostles and of the Church. Jesus showed us what this forgiveness was like and what it meant when he healed the paralytic. The Church declares the absolution of sins; she miraculously raises up a man paralysed by his wrong-doing. She performs an act of spiritual resurrection; it is her risen Lord acting through her. It was the risen Christ who, on the evening of the first Easter Day, conferred on his Apostles, and through them on the Church, the power and the mission of forgiveness. The Lord said to them: 'Peace be unto you: as my Father hath sent me, even so send I you.' The Father sent the Son who on earth has power to forgive sins, and the Son likewise sends the Church with the same power. 'And, when he had said this, he breathed on them, and saith unto them, Receive ye the Holy Ghost: whose soever sins ye remit, they are remitted unto them; and whose soever sins ye retain, they are retained' (John 20.22-3).

This is the only instance in the Gospel in which Christ performs this act of breathing on them to signify the gift of the Holy Ghost. In the Greek version of the Old Testament the same word 'breathe' is used in the same sense three times. Firstly at the creation of man when the Lord 'breathed into his nostrils the breath of life; and man became a living soul' (Gen. 2.7). Then in the account of the raising of the son of the widow of Zarephath where we read of how Elijah 'stretched himself upon the child[1] three times, and

---

[1] *Translator's note:* So AV. The Septuagint reads 'breathed into the child'.

cried unto the Lord, and said, O Lord my God, I pray thee, let this child's soul come into him again' (I Kings 17.21). Lastly, in Ezekiel's vision, the prophet is to cry 'Come from the four winds, O breath [or spirit], and breathe upon these slain, that they may live' (Ezek. 37.9). In these three texts the breath of the Spirit is connected with life, healing, and resurrection. The Lord breathes in order to create a living being. Elijah breathes in order to restore life to a dying boy. Ezekiel invokes the breath of the Spirit in order to raise up again the people of God. It is in this context of healing, resurrection, restoration to life, and re-creation that we must see Christ's action; the gift he bestows upon his disciples is one of spiritual resurrection. The Church receives the power to make men live again spiritually by the remission of sins. Because sin deprives us of the true life received at the Creation and renewed in Jesus Christ, because it reduces us to the state of being near to death, or that of dry bones, we need the very breath of the Holy Spirit to revive us, dead bodies that we are. The Church must use this gift of the recreative breath which Christ transmitted to the Apostles. The gift received by the Apostles on the evening of Easter Day is not to be identified with the gift of proclaiming the Good News. Christ's promise first to Peter, and then to all the Apostles, according to which whatever the Church binds on earth will be bound in heaven and whatever she looses will be loosed (Matt. 16.19; 18.18), concerns the whole apostolic ministry. It is with a view to the totality of this ministry that the Apostles receive at Pentecost the fulness of the Holy Ghost. But here a particular gift is concerned: the Apostles receive a holy Spirit, a promise, a mission, a special ministry. This ministry is an aspect of the power of the keys, which ought to be understood as including the whole of the Church's task of setting men free. This gift, promise, mission, and ministry is the power of absolution. It is not a question of the ministry of preaching only, but of a word and an act which operate what they signify. Christ did not say that their sins would be remitted who by faith appropriated to themselves the promise of forgiveness when it was preached to them. He said:

'Whose soever sins ye *remit*, they are *remitted* unto them.' We have here an example of a sacramental act. According to the theology of the Early Fathers of the Church, it is a sacrament when, on the promise of Jesus Christ, the Church believes that God acts conjointly and effectually in a sign which she addresses to the believer. One may say that all the conditions which make the Lord's Supper and Baptism sacraments—according to Reformed theology itself—are to be found present here. The Heidelberg Catechism thus defines the sacraments: 'They are visible signs and seals instituted by God to the end that, by their use, he may make us the more clearly understand and seal in us the promise of the Gospel, namely that because of the unique sacrifice of Jesus Christ accomplished on the Cross, he grants us by grace forgiveness of sins and eternal life.'[1]

In the act of absolution we find this particular, concrete, visible character which is required of a sacrament. Calvin quotes one of St Augustine's definitions of a sacrament in order to prove that penance cannot be so termed, since it does not fulfil the condition of material visibility. 'The same writer [Augustine] says in another place, "A sacrament therefore is so called, because one thing is seen, another is understood in it. That which is seen has corporeal form; that which is understood has spiritual fruit." '[2] Calvin is here following a definition that is far too Scholastic. The concrete character of the sacrament does not imply a matter in the ordinarily accepted sense, but a particular act which entails the action of God himself. It should be added that the imposition of hands appears to have formed part of the sacrament of absolution from a very early date. The second condition, much more important for Reformed theology, namely that the sacrament should have been instituted by God, is also fulfilled in the case of absolution. Christ himself, after his Resurrection, explicitly mentioned this particular ministry as a part of the whole ministry of the Church. The third condition, that it should be related to the

[1] *Heidelberg Catechism*, XXV, Question 66.
[2] *Institutes*, 1560, Bk. IV, Ch. XIX, Para. 15.

unique sacrifice of Christ on the Cross, is also met in absolution, since absolution bears witness to the remission of sins, which can be accorded today only because of the death and resurrection of our Lord. Finally, the fourth sacramental characteristic, that of efficacy, we have already recognized to be present: absolution is a sign that God grants by grace forgiveness of sins and eternal life.

We must now consider the spiritual profit to be derived from having the sign of absolution in addition to the simple preaching of forgiveness. It is true that there are many who do not see the need for adding to faith in the mercy of God a sign of remission and absolution. Is it not enough to believe in the forgiveness for it to be granted to you? It must be said that such an argument does not only weaken the value of the sign of absolution, but cuts at the root of every kind of sacramental life. Is it not then also enough to believe that one is in the Church and in communion with Jesus Christ? What need is there of Baptism and the Lord's Supper, the signs of entry and fellowship? This is a matter of the necessary distinction between the announcement or preaching of the Word of God and the sacramental signs. In the Word, written or preached, Christ's promise is announced to us. We may, by faith and prayer, which are the works of the Spirit in us, make this promise into a reality. I can hear a sermon on the infinite mercy of God, and effectually experience forgiveness, if I receive the words of the preacher in true faith and in a spirit of prayer. But it is possible for me not to understand or not really to listen to the message of liberation. I may doubt whether it is in very truth addressed to me personally; I may believe myself to be either not sinful enough, or, on the contrary, too great a sinner, for it to be applied to me. In a sacrament God in a sense compels the faith of the believer, however weak it be, and accomplishes for him and in him the work signified by the sacrament, far beyond all he can ask or think. In the sign of absolution the mercy of God is not only proposed to faith and prayer as a realizable promise, but sins are actually and personally remitted by the Church, acting on the authority of the Apostles and of Jesus Christ. The sacrament of absolution therefore effectually confers what it signifies. God's Word announcing the promise of mercy made by Jesus Christ must be made concrete in the sign of absolution; and the believer must realize that the remission of sins is not only a hope, but an actual fact to which he can hold fast with all his faith.[1]

The prodigal son in the parable, when he came to himself, told himself that his father would accept him at least as a hired servant if he returned home. He was persuaded that his father would overlook his life of profligacy and debauchery and provide food and lodging for his son. So there was forming in his mind a repentance not unmixed with self-interest. The forgiveness he imagined went no further than the ordinary duty of a father. Nevertheless his decision to return showed his faith: he knew that his father would forgive him. Yet his faith was tinged with anxiety, envisaging as he did the conditions which would make such compassion possible. He must propose that he be treated as one of the servants. His meditation was bringing him to the certainty that a father could not shut the door in his son's face, even though he had greatly sinned against him. He believed in his father's goodness, but he could not believe in the possibility of being truly recognized as a son in his father's house. If we are really conscious of our sin, we must feel the same anxiety. Otherwise we become accustomed to our wrongdoing and begin to take God's mercy as a matter of course. One often meets this lack of any real conviction of sin and any real yearning for the mercy of God, particularly among those who say that the promise of the Word of God is

[1] I have already pointed out that the sacramental value of absolution was recognized by Luther. The place accorded in the *Little Catechism* to the chapter on confession, between those on Baptism and the Lord's Supper, is one more proof of this. The *Great Catechism* puts this chapter after the others. In the *Little Catechism*, to the question: 'What is confession?' the catechumen replies: 'Confession comprises two things. Firstly, one must confess one's sins; secondly one must receive absolution or pardon from the confessor as from God Himself, and doubt not, but firmly believe, that by this means our sins are forgiven before God in heaven.' (See my Conclusion, p. 147).

sufficient, and that all that is required is to believe in it. It becomes too easy to believe that a general promise must necessarily apply to each and every individual. Such a prodigal, sure of his father's indulgent good-nature and of the success of his plan, will have no great qualms about returning to his family. There are others, however, in whom the general nature of the promise may arouse anguish of mind, if not a guilt-complex. Filled with the feeling of their own unworthiness, more perhaps than with a sense of God's holiness, they do not believe themselves capable of finding peace, and live in a state of conscious or unconscious fear. They are prodigal sons who would rather die in a far country than return to their father's house, where they think there is no longer any place for them. The parable reveals a quite different spiritual attitude. Anxiously, but convinced of his father's compassion, severe though he may be, the son has taken the road home. 'But when he was yet a great way off, his father saw him, and had compassion, and ran, and fell on his neck, and kissed him. And the son said unto him, Father, I have sinned against heaven, and in thy sight, and am no more worthy to be called thy son' (Luke 15.20-1). The Father does not wait for our repentance, our faith, or our prayers to bring us into his presence. In the distance of our just anxiety he sees us, he has compassion, he comes in person to us in the haste of his love. No word—only the sign of the kiss. In the certainty of this direct and personal contact with the Father we can make true and sincere confession of our sin. 'But the father said to his servants, Bring forth the best robe, and put it on him; and put a ring on his hand, and shoes on his feet: and bring hither the fatted calf, and kill it; and let us eat, and be merry: for this my son was dead, and is alive again; he was lost, and is found' (Luke 15.22-4). The father has heard his son's confession, but he makes no comment, no reproach, no sermon, 'but he says to his servants . . .' In answer to our confession the Lord does not lecture us on morality. He does not preach mercy to us. He announces no promise of forgiveness to us—but he orders his servants, his Church, to give a sign of his love and his joy. They are to clothe

the pardoned sinner with the unmerited robe of righteousness, to put on his finger the ring of the renewed covenant, and to put on his feet 'the preparation of the gospel of peace' (Eph. 6.15). Accepted once more into his Father's house, the sinner can share in the joy of the eucharistic feast. He was dead, and is alive again; he was lost, and is found.

At the end of the Epistle of St James, Christians are exhorted in the following terms: 'Confess therefore your sins one to another, and pray one for another, that ye may be healed. The supplication of a righteous man availeth much in its working. Elijah was a man of like passions with us, and he prayed fervently that it might not rain; and it rained not on the earth for three years and six months. And he prayed again; and the heaven gave rain, and the earth brought forth her fruit. My brethren, if any among you do err from the truth, and one convert him; let him know, that he which converteth a sinner from the error of his way shall save a soul from death, and shall cover a multitude of sins' (James 5.16-20, RV). The context of this exhortation to confession is of great importance for an understanding of the spirit in which it ought to be done and of the form it ought to take. St James has just been writing of the ministry of healing. If anyone is sick, he must call the elders of the Church, who are to pray for him after having anointed him with oil in the name of the Lord. The prayer of faith will save him that is sick, and the Lord will raise him up; and if he has committed sins they will be forgiven him (James 5.14-5). 'Confess *therefore* your sins . . .', our text continues. It is, then, in the special case of physical healing that confession is here envisaged. The Apostle establishes a relationship between sin and disease; not that the Bible considers every disease to be the consequence of a particular sin; but there is a certain connection between disease and the indifference or the general revolt of man against God, which we call sin. The ministry of healing involves, along with the prayer of faith, the imposition of hands, and unction, a confession of sins; for the effects of this ministry consist not only in a possible physical or psychical healing, but also in the remission of sins committed and confessed. Thus the practice of confession is to be seen as having a place within the framework of the apostolic ministry of the Church, and, here, in the particular framework of the ministry of healing. It is an ecclesiastical ministry belonging to the Christian community, represented by its elders or ministers. This passage about confession has too often been interpreted in the sense of a fraternal sharing of the difficulties of the Christian life. Under the pretext of an imperfectly understood theology of universal priesthood, and of the unique mediation of Jesus Christ interpreted in an anti-ecclesiastical sense, the view of the confession of sins as the concern of the whole Church has been lost. For St James confession has the same meaning as we have noted elsewhere: whether private or public, it is a sacramental act of the community.

Confession, and the intercessory prayer which is its sequel, are aimed at healing, which we are to understand in the sense of a resurrection of the whole man by the Lord. Confession and the prayer for the healing of the person are here envisaged as effective signs, of great power. The effectual fervent prayer of a righteous man availeth much (James 5.16). What are we to understand by this righteousness and fervour? In St James' conception of the Christian life, the righteousness of the righteous man is to be understood as a total commitment to obedience to Christ, a moral and ascetic obedience. This means that the ministry of healing, confession, and intercession calls for great vigilance and obedience on the part of the Church, by both clergy and laity, although the effectiveness of the ministry does not depend on this. God is faithful, he heals, forgives, and answers prayer infinitely beyond all that we ask or think; his action is free, and does not depend on our obedience, but he nevertheless requires of his Church the vigilance and obedience which must signify and fortify her faith. Indeed, it is always faith which God answers, even in the sacrament. Fervour is not the psychological over-heating it is too often thought to be, but a total self-giving in the act of faith and intercession. Our whole being must be given to God in calm

57

confidence: body, mind, and spirit. We are not to imitate the prophets of Baal, who leaped about the altar, and who 'cut themselves . . . with knives and lancets, till the blood gushed out upon them', thinking thus to attract the attention of their god. We must be like Elijah, who believed in the truth of the God of Abraham, Isaac, and Israel, and who did all things at his Word. To his instant prayer God replied with the fire that consumed the sacrifice, and then gave rain (I Kings 18). This fervour may involve an ascetic discipline, namely fasting, which gives expression to the insistence of the prayer. So when the Church engages in this ministry of healing, confession, and intercession she must not neglect her spiritual discipline. The requirement concerning righteousness and fervour is especially important for her ministers. Men like the Curé d'Ars, or Pastor Blumhardt, are typical examples of the effectiveness of the ministry of healing, confession, and intercession, exercised by fervent righteous men.[1]

The ministry of confession is considered by St James to be a solemn and important charge. What it really means is the bringing back of the sinner who has lost his way and strayed far from the truth. To accomplish this mission is to share in Christ's work of resurrection; it is to save a soul from death. We have already seen in the institution by the resurrected Christ of the ministry of absolution this character of renewal of life, signified by the Lord's breathing. The ministry of confession, furthermore, makes possible the covering of 'a multitude of sins'. In accordance with his promise, God consents to see no more and to blot out the

---

[1] See E. Grin, *Jean-Christophe Blumhardt*, Labor et Fides, Geneva, 1952. Blumhardt rediscovered the power of confession and absolution: see pp. 136-7. The re-awakening of his parish dates from the introduction of confession.

'He knelt down,' he writes of one of his first penitents, 'and *I gave him absolution by the imposition of hands*. When he stood up he was transformed: his face shone with joy and gratitude. . . .'

'The numbers coming to receive this ministration are so great that I am seeing them from seven in the morning until late at night. . . .'

'Several times over, I have given absolution. I thought it right to repeat the act, so broken were their hearts. I have brought back a goodly number of people . . .' (pp. 60, 61, 62).

confessed and forgiven wrongdoing. He clothes the sinner with the garment of righteousness which covers the multitude of his sins.

I have spoken of the laying on of hands which accompanied the reconciliation of sinners in the early Church. There is a possible allusion to it in the First Epistle to Timothy: 'Lay hands suddenly on no man,' writes the Apostle, 'neither be partaker of other men's sins: keep thyself pure' (I Tim. 5.22). The context of this quotation seems to favour the interpretation of the gesture as a sign of absolution and reconciliation. It is, in fact, concerned not with the ordination of ministers, but with 'some men's sins' (24-5). To reconcile them lightly and unconditionally with the Christian community by laying hands on them would be to share in their sin. Here again we have an indication of the possible communion of the Church in sin, through carelessness, complacency, or indifference. The ministry of confession must be exercised with circumspection and prudence. To give absolution in God's name heedlessly and lightly is really to consider the sin confessed as being of little moment, to excuse it, to do Satan's work for him. The confessor must keep himself pure. He must not let himself slip into an easy complacency which might amount to complicity in the sin. His ministry would then be the occasion of his own downfall.

The few examples of the confession of sins which are recorded in the Bible are generally public confessions. Thus in the New Testament we have the case of those who came to the River Jordan to John the Baptist, and who 'were baptized of him, confessing their sins' (Matt. 3.6; Mark 1.5). In the Acts of the Apostles we read that in Ephesus 'many that believed came, and confessed, and shewed their deeds', either to St Paul or to the Church (Acts 19.18). The public confession of scandalous wrongdoing always has its value in the Church, but the public confession of private difficulties may do serious harm. The weaker members of the community may be perturbed and even scandalized if such a confession is not made with every circumstance of Christian prudence. All the same, confession must not be turned into a private mystery; it may sometimes be desirable and useful to disclose an intimate personal difficulty to several brethren in the Church, providing it is done in a spirit of discipline and obedience, for it may give rise to an unhealthy tendency to talk about oneself which would be profitable to nobody.

The first forms for 'private penance' appear in the West only towards the middle of the fifth century, and it was not until the Fourth Lateran Council, in 1215, that the discipline of private confession finally took the form it has today in the Roman Church. Formerly, the most usual practice was the sacramental and public reconciliation of serious and scandalous sinners who had been excommunicated. St Gregory of Nyssa (d. 394) states that the sins thus dealt with were the three major ones of apostasy, adultery, and murder.[1] The reconciliation took place chiefly at the end of Lent, on Maundy Thursday. The penance imposed might often extend over a period of three years. For abortion, one could be excommunicated for as much as ten years, and for murder, eleven; in the case of homicide by chance-medley, three years' abstention from communion was advised. These details are given by St Basil.[2]

Private confession to a priest already existed, however, in the early centuries, although the only sacramental rite was the public reconciliation. We see from Socrates' account that it existed at Constantinople in the fourth century (under the episcopate of Nectarius, 381-97). 'A woman of noble family coming to the penitentiary, made a general confession of those sins she had committed since her baptism: and the presbyter enjoined fasting and prayer continually, that together with the acknowledgement of error, she might have to show works also meet for repentance.'[3] It is interesting to note the meaning of the satisfaction as indicated by this quotation: the fasting and prayer are, like the confession, signs of repentance and not acts done in order to merit forgiveness.

The fact that the sacrament of private penance as it is understood

[1] *Epistola canonica*, P.G., Vol. XLV, Col. 221-36.
[2] P.G., Vol. XXXII, Col. 664f.   [3] See p. 31, n.3.

today does not appear in the early writings, cannot therefore be taken as meaning that private confession did not exist. We may say that public and private confession existed side by side in the Church from the earliest times. Public confession, when it took place, was always preceded by a private confession, but the sacrament of reconciliation was administered publicly. Moreover, this public and sacramental reconciliation did not necessarily involve public confession. Along with the sinners who were making public confession of their sins, there were Christians who had made their confession in secret only, either to the bishop or to a penitentiary priest, and who could therefore also receive the public sign of their reconciliation with the Church. Rather than an evolution from public to private confession, we should note simply that the sacramental rite of public reconciliation gradually became private sacramental absolution. St Leo the Great, Bishop of Rome from 440 to 461, wrote in 459 to the bishops established in Campania, Samnium, and Picenum, where confessors were betraying the secrecy of the confessional: 'I prescribe that that presumption *contrary to the apostolic rule*, which I have lately learned is being committed by certain illicit usurpers, be utterly banished. Clearly, concerning the penitence which is demanded by the faithful, one must not read publicly the notes of a written confession on the nature of each individual sin, since it suffices that the state of conscience be indicated *in secret confession* to the priests alone [i.e. to the bishops, the word *sacerdos* applying only to the bishop until the middle of the fifth century]. Although one must praise that plenitude of faith which, through fear of God, does not shrink from blushing before men, yet since the sins of all those who seek penance are not of such a nature that they do not fear to have them published abroad, it is necessary to desist from this custom, of which one cannot approve, lest many be put off from availing themselves of the remedies of penance, either through shame or through fear of seeing revealed to their enemies deeds for which they may be subject to the action of the law. Moreover, that confession is sufficient which is made firstly to

God, and then also to the priest, who prays for the sins of the penitents. Only then will many allow themselves to be summoned to penance, if the conscience of him who is confessing is not to be revealed to the ears of the people.'[1]

St Leo commends the public confession which some may make in 'the plenitude of faith', but he condemns the betrayal of secrecy by confessors. The bishop, as head of the community, is still the sole confessor, because he exercises the ministry of penance and of sacramental public reconciliation. As early as the third century, however, there existed in certain countries the office of penitentiary priest, to whom was delegated by the bishop the duty of hearing confessions. St Leo makes it clear that public and private confession existed side by side, the latter not excluding public penance and reconciliation. This great Latin theologian points the way for our own churches. Would it not be possible to envisage, in addition to the possibility of public confession in exceptional cases, in a restricted community, the practice of a liturgy of reconciliation, during Lent—on Maundy Thursday, for example —in which all those believers who wished to manifest publicly their state of sin and to receive the visible assurance of their reintegration into the full communion of the Church might take part? The act might be inaugurated at the beginning of Lent by the liturgy of Ash Wednesday, in which prayers would be offered for victory over the Devil (exorcism), due preparation having been made by a serious examination of conscience and private confession. Some essays of this sort are a feature of the Catholic liturgical revival. In these days when we have lost the sense of the gravity of sin, such liturgies, with their emphasis on the life of the community, can be a great help towards reawakening that sense in us, and towards the realization of the joy of forgiveness.

St Thomas Aquinas distinguishes three sorts of confession still practised in his day: solemn penance, public (non-ritual)

[1] See Migne, *Patrologiae cursus completus*, Paris, 1846, Vol. 54, Col. 1,210.

penance, and private penance.[1] One may wonder if the complete disappearance of public penance is not a result of the weakening of community life and the growth of individualism in the Church. From the time of the Renaissance onwards the sense of collective responsibility in sin was little felt, and then belief in the objective struggle of the community against Satan became less and less. Certain Pietist sects alone rediscovered this sense, but in a distorted form, through being cut off from the main tradition. The Bishops' Pontifical still contains the rites, but only as pious relics of the past.[2]

To sum up, private confession and public confession existed side by side in the Church from the earliest times, though neither was obligatory. Public confession may even be said to have been exceptional in the early Church. Only the 'exomologesis', the public confession of guilt with a view to reconciliation, without a detailed disclosure of the sins committed, but preceded by a secret confession, was generally practised and sometimes even required of those guilty of serious and notorious sins.

The following is the decree of the Lateran Council (1215), which defined the practice of confession in the West (Canon 21):

'Every Christian, of either sex, who has come to years of discretion, is to confess his sins to his own priest at least once a year, to carry out to the best of his ability the penance imposed upon him, and devoutly to receive, at Easter at least, the Sacrament of the Eucharist; unless, for good cause, on the advice of the priest, he defers until later the receiving of this Sacrament. Anyone not conforming to this prescription is to be excluded from the Church, and in case of death will not receive ecclesiastical burial.

'This ordinance is to be published frequently in the Churches

---

[1] *Commentary on the Sentences*, dist. XIV, q. 1, a.5.
Solemn penance includes all the rites of reintegration of notorious sinners. Non-ritual public penance generally takes the form of a pilgrimage. Neither of these necessarily involves a detailed public confession. They are really forms of public 'satisfaction'.

[2] *Pontificale romanum*, 'Of the public expulsion of penitents from the Church in the fourth Feria in Lent', and 'Of the reconciliation of penitents which takes place in the fifth Feria of the Lord's Supper'.

so that none may be able to plead the excuse of ignorance. If anyone, from valid motives, desires to confess to another priest, he is to ask and obtain the permission of his own priest, without which permission the second priest cannot loose or bind him.

'The priest must be prudent and wise, know how to pour wine and oil on the wounds, to discern the circumstances of the sin and the state of mind of the sinner, in order to be able to determine what advice to give, what remedy to apply, and what means to adopt to heal the sick person.

'He is to take great care not to betray the sinner through some imprudent word or sign. If he needs to consult a more instructed person, let him do it prudently without indicating any name. The priest who discloses a wrong confided to him in confession will be not only deposed from his priestly office, but also confined in a closed monastery, there to do penance to the end of his life.'[1]

This juridical decree has unfortunately led the faithful to practise only the necessary spiritual minimum (Easter Confession and Communion), with dire results as regards the practice both of Confession and of Communion. When the Church is reduced to fixing a necessary minimum, it is perhaps a sign that she has lost faith in the attraction of the treasures of grace.

[1] *Dict. Théol. cath.*, Vol. XII, 1, Col. 949-50.

CHAPTER FOUR

CONFESSION, DIRECTION, AND OPEN-HEARTEDNESS[1]

THE theological revival of the idea of the Church has in recent years increasingly taken the form of a revival in the liturgical and community life of the parish. There has been a realization of the extent to which Christian life has been reduced to an individualistic practice of prayer and personal obedience. Our immediate predecessors in the faith laid great stress on the individual Christian life, and the importance of this contribution by the nineteenth century to her spiritual life must continually be restated by the Church if the growth of community life is not to lead to formalistic ritualism and ecclesiasticism. But the deepening understanding of the Church as the Body of Christ obliges us to consider our personal Christian life as dependent upon the life of the community.

Our spiritual life is nourished and fulfilled in the communion of saints. Increasing attention is being paid today to this article of the Creed. Not only does our inner life need communion with the Holy One (*Sanctus*) and the holy things (*sancta*: God's Word, the Sacraments, worship, prayer), but the communion of saints (*sancti*) is also indispensable to its continued growth. The communion of saints means first of all the certainty that beyond appearances, beyond the sympathies or antipathies which may hide from us the inner reality of the members of the Body of Christ, there exists in the parish or in the Christian community an ontological and vital relationship between those whom God has called to be saints, that is to say those who are baptized and live

[1] I am indebted for the substance of this chapter to Brother Roger's book, *Introduction à la vie communautaire*, Labor et Fides, Geneva, 1944. In particular, on spiritual direction, see pp. 36-8, 74-85.

by faith. The communion of saints is a life-stream circulated by the Holy Spirit through the members of Christ's Body. We might compare this theological reality with the circulation of the blood in the human body. To listen together to God's Word, to recite the same Creed, to receive the eucharistic bread and wine, is to enter into a mysterious but real communion. When they come back from the Holy Table the communicants find themselves in a new existential situation. Each one no longer belongs to himself, but as Christ has entered into each in order to make all things new, so each is now bound to his neighbour, whether he realizes it or not, in a manner which is not found in any human society, even the most sacred, in any human intimacy, in any human love. This hidden and intimate communion within the local community extends also to the universal Church. The Eucharist more than anything else ought to make us aware of the essential bond that exists among all those who form part of the Body of Christ. It is a communion which reaches out also in the dimensions of time. It is a bond which binds us to all those who have preceded us in the Church militant on earth and who now enjoy the peace of Paradise as they wait with us for resurrection and glory. Lastly, this communion includes also those whom God, in the mystery of his predestination, is preparing for a decisive encounter with Jesus Christ. 'The mystery . . . that the Gentiles should be fellowheirs, and of the same body, and partakers of his promise in Christ by the gospel' (Eph. 3.3, 6). So the community of saints will not allow us to be restrictive. It deploys our love according to the dimensions of that of Christ himself. We are 'able to comprehend with all saints what is the breadth, and length, and depth, and height; and to know the love of Christ, which passeth knowledge' (Eph. 3.18-19). In the communion of saints we are filled with all the fulness of God, the fulness of love which implies suffering as well as joy. Thus St Paul is able to say: 'Whether one member suffer, all the members suffer with it; or one member be honoured, all the members rejoice with it' (I Cor. 12.26). With the Christians of the whole Church militant here on earth we suffer from the sin, the weaknesses, and the trials endured by the Body of Christ. But also we can rejoice in the victories won by Christ in his followers on earth, and those which he has won in the lives of his saints who are now honoured with the vision of God and his angels.

This concept of the ontological unity of the Body of Christ in the communion of saints was an essential article of faith in the primitive Church. The salvation, resurrection, and glorification of the Christian are not a purely private affair, dependent only on the personal faith of each individual. There is a solidarity in sin and in faith, which makes us carry each other along in our march towards Jesus Christ. We are responsible one for another, and we can aid and support each other by intercession. If we can 'run with patience the race that is set before us, looking unto Jesus', it is because we are compassed about with the great cloud of witnesses (Heb. 12.1). We are in some sort drawn onwards by the 'general assembly and church of the first-born' (Heb. 12.23). We are dependent on the faith, the dedication, the patience of those whom it was not God's will to make perfect without us: all those witnesses and martyrs whose obedience, whose sufferings, and whose trials are described in the Epistle to the Hebrews (Heb. 11).

The conviction of the reality of the communion of saints was so strong in the early Church that at Corinth there were some Christians who went so far as to have themselves baptized for persons who were dead, presumably catechumens who had died before their baptism. Without giving his approval to this practice, but also without criticizing it, the Apostle uses it as an argument in support of belief in the resurrection of the dead. If one has oneself baptized for the dead, one must believe in their resurrection. 'Else what shall they do which are baptized for the dead, if the dead rise not at all? why are they then baptized for the dead?' (I Cor. 15.29). This practice, to which St Paul refers in passing, gives some idea of the intensity of community life in the Church and the assurance of the reality of the communion of saints which Christians had at that time. So truly one in Christ are the saints that it was felt that through intercession the sacrament could have a retrospective effect on those who could no longer receive it. The baptism of living Christians could be effective for the resurrection of Christians who had died without baptism. We do not of course share this view of the practice of baptism—a practice which receives no support from St Paul—but it is an extreme and somewhat distorted sign of a real and fervent faith in the communion of saints.

If one believes in the way I have indicated in the reality of the communion of saints, one is also called to witness to its existence. The same is true of every aspect of our Christian life. We are holy, called to be saints, called to sanctification. We are called upon to become in our existence what we are in essence, that is, in Jesus Christ. The same is true of the Church, the Christian community. She is the Body of Christ, made up of the community of saints; but that which *is* essentially, must *exist* externally. Everything that will show forth the Church as a living community must be developed. That is why St Paul exhorts the Corinthians, to whom he reveals the mystery of the unity of the Church 'that ye all speak the same thing . . . that ye be perfectly joined together in the same mind and in the same judgement'. The unity of confession in the faith, of theology, must be complemented by psychological unity.

Open-heartedness towards one another among the members of one and the same Church is one of the most important factors making for the realization in existence of the essential unity of the community. For this open-heartedness to be a practical reality, the local Church must not be too numerous. As we move towards an ecumenical understanding of the Church, we must also seek to form small local parishes. If this is impossible for reasons of tradition or administration, we must work for the break-up of parishes into districts. In such small local communities openness between individuals can be made real in the sharing in common of the spiritual wealth of all, as well as the sharing of the difficulties encountered and the victories won. This is not confession properly so-called, but a simple exchange which saves the individual from becoming unhealthily wrapped up in the cult of his own personality.

I have said that in certain cases the confession of a wrong or a difficulty to several people may be the only means of snatching from Satan his last weapons; but this exceptional confession can only be practised in discipline and obedience to a spiritual director.[1] Anarchy in the practice of confession, apart from the fact that it may pander to a morbid need to attract attention and make oneself loved, may be disturbing to the weaker members of the Church. This type of confession must not in any case be made publicly, but in private to several persons. The practice of sharing as an aid to mutual open-heartedness can become a habit which finds in itself its own satisfaction. One can waste on it time and energy which ought to be devoted to the service of Christ. In order that the sharing should not turn into introspective analysis, it must always have as its aim the spiritual healing of the person and the deepening of the community consciousness of the Church. It must be accompanied by spiritual direction. The aim, in fact, of sharing one's difficulties is not solely to rid oneself of a burden which others will then carry in prayer, but to find the way to liberation from it by the help of the Holy Ghost. A simple psychological release has a limited value if it does not take place within the context of a real pastoral ministry to the soul.

Spiritual direction or the cure of souls is a seeking after the leading of the Holy Spirit in a given psychological and spiritual situation.[2] It means nothing other than the direction of a life by the Holy Spirit. The Church as such exercises the ministry of direction

[1] St Ambrose urges us to be frank about ourselves in these words: 'Ask the Church, therefore, to pray for you; there is nothing in this that need make you blush, unless it be for failing to admit your guilt, since we are all sinners' (*De paenitentia*, Bk. II, Ch. XVI).

[2] The distinction often made—not without an axe to grind, one feels— by a certain school of Protestant pastoral theology between the cure of souls and spiritual direction, seems artificial. According to this view the cure of souls is the preaching of God's Word in private to an individual, while spiritual direction involves the intervention of psychological factors. A verdict is therefore given in favour of the cure of souls as against spiritual direction. Is it really possible to conceive of preaching, however objective, which does not involve psychological expression of some kind? The pastoral care of souls especially, aimed as it is at particular persons with particular spiritual and psychological problems, cannot do

through her preaching, her liturgy, and the personal witness of her members. But the term 'spiritual direction' is more particularly used to designate the search for the direction of the Holy Spirit in which a Christian engages with the help of a director. Spiritual direction tries to rise above the level of the purely psychological. It is not to be confused with psychoanalysis. Director and directed together seek, in prayer and obedience to God's Word, the leading of the Holy Spirit. It is in this sense that direction is called spiritual, and not because of its being concerned only with so-called spiritual matters or with the soul. The truth is that the Holy Spirit seeks to order the whole of our physical, psychological, and spiritual life in accordance with God's will for us. Spiritual direction is more effective when the method employed is what one might call non-directive, to use a term current in scientific psychology. This method consists in the director listening and refusing to intervene in an authoritarian and categorical manner, so as the better to allow the person being directed to discover for himself, by prayer and meditation enlightened by the Word of God, what the will of the Holy Spirit is for him. Christian spiritual direction, so far from seeking to impose itself, tends thus to render itself superfluous. This remark must not be taken as condoning the timidity in direction which one meets with in some pastors, and which is really a mistaken interpretation of the humility of the ministry. In certain cases the director may make a definite decision, if he is sure that it is God's

without some form of psychological expression. Listening, understanding and having compassion inevitably involve psychology. The giving of pastoral advice cannot be confined purely and simply to the preaching of the Word. It must be expressed with the particular needs and weaknesses of the individual in mind—that is to say, psychologically. On the other hand spiritual direction, as we shall see more clearly later, is of necessity based on the Bible; otherwise it ceases to be spiritual, to become merely an analysis followed by psychological advice. I am therefore led to the conclusion that the cure of souls and spiritual direction are identical, finding nothing in the history of pastoral theology that would justify any differentiation between them. If it is held that the only distinction is one of emphasis, and no claim is made for the 'spiritual purity' of the cure of souls to the exclusion of spiritual direction, then I am willing to agree. In that case it is simply a matter of the definition of terms

will and that the person being directed is of a hesitant nature and
incapable of making a decision for himself; but this must remain
the exception rather than the rule. This is why I do not use the
term 'direction of conscience', which seems unsuitable to our
subject, since it gives the impression that the person directed
must abdicate his own will in order to obey his director. St
John the Baptist is the type of the spiritual director, since all
his preaching, his exhortation, his ministry of confession and
direction aimed at the preparation of the way of the Lord. His
words should be taken to heart by every spiritual director: 'A
man can receive nothing, except it be given him from heaven.
You yourselves bear me witness, that I said, I am not the Christ,
but that I am sent before him. He that hath the bride is the
bridegroom: but the friend of the bridegroom, which standeth and
heareth him, rejoiceth greatly because of the bridegroom's voice:
this my joy is therefore fulfilled. He must increase, but I must
decrease' (John 3.27-30). One thing the spiritual director must
be sure about above all: that he can do absolutely nothing if the
grace is not given him to listen patiently and to say the word that
will allow the Holy Spirit to impose his direction. Without this
gift from on high, the director can only practise psychological
analysis, or else impose his own theological or moral points of
view. He must be very conscious that he has been sent before
Christ, and that it is to him that he must lead those who look
to him for guidance. He that has the bride, the Church, is the
bridegroom, Jesus Christ. The director must rid himself completely of any spirit of possessiveness, authority, or exclusive
intimacy in regard to those whom he directs. This is a delicate
and difficult matter, for the whole tendency of our nature, and the
great temptation of the pastor, is to cultivate this possessiveness,
this authoritarianism, and this desire for admiration, intimacy,
and affection. The spiritual director is only the bridegroom's
friend; he is not the bridegroom. His task is to stand near Christ,
contemplating his Person, meditating on his teaching, and interceding with him for all those who are entrusted to him. His

greatest joy ought to be to hear the bridegroom's voice, to discern what is his will for those in his charge. The joy of the spiritual director will be fulfilled when he sees Christ growing in those whom he has been trying to lead towards him, and feels himself gradually surpassed by the working of the Holy Ghost in them, so that his services become more and more unnecessary to them. 'He must increase, but I must decrease.'

So spiritual direction, more than mutual sharing, manifests the working of the Holy Ghost in the lives of Christians. It has a more definitely transcendent character than the simple exchange of difficulties of which sharing consists. While the latter may never rise above the level of human dialogue, of psychological release without any real seeking after God's will, direction perfects it by giving a meaning to its sincerity, which can only have value when it is directed towards spiritual healing. Direction is the search for this healing. If direction is to be allowed to become the transcendent action of the Holy Spirit, it is in general better that it should not be mutual, otherwise there is a risk of its becoming once more a mere sharing. This concerns pastors in particular.

Nevertheless, since spiritual direction must avail itself of human speech and counsel, sober and inspired though these may be, there is always a danger that it may not show forth the guidance of the Holy Spirit. If, through some failure on the part of the director or the person directed, the spirit of prayer or of obedience is not strong enough, direction is capable of being too human, when it will not bring perfect discipleship and joy. Even in the best conditions, the humanity of the director, his manner of listening and speaking, set up a screen in front of the Person of Christ, even when they reveal him.[1]

[1] My intention has been to confine myself to the cure of souls and spiritual direction in so far as they relate to the need for sincerity between Christians and to confession. My purpose is not to deal exhaustively with spiritual direction. For this the reader may consult the following: J.-D. Benoit, *Direction spirituelle et protestantisme. Etude sur la légitimité d'une direction protestante*, Alcan, Paris, 1940; H. Asmussen, *Die Seelsorge*, Kaiser, Munich; E. Thurneysen, *Die Lehre von der Seelsorge*, Evangelischer Verlag A. G., Zurich, 1946.

Confession properly so-called, and the sign of absolution, show better than anything else that the Lord alone is director of our sinful lives. Confession is neither sharing nor directing. It is not a mutual exchange of difficulties and problems by two Christians, nor is it a seeking of God's advice upon some question raised by our life.

On the part of the penitent who comes to confess, confession implies essentially a waiting upon God's mercy, his forgiveness, his absolution. He must prepare himself by self-examination, and present himself before God in the presence of a minister of the Church in order to tell him of his misery and his sin. And he must come with his eyes fixed only on God; as in the love of Christ himself, there is no room here for any trace of self-interest. Just as we cannot bear to keep a secret from someone we love, from the man or woman who shares our daily life, so we cannot appear in God's sight without telling him the most intimate secrets of our sinful hearts. But God knows our sinfulness far better than we do ourselves, even before we are ready to reveal it to him. This, though true, in no wise detracts from the value of confession. Such, indeed, is the case with every expression of our Christian life. God knows our needs and our prayers before we express them, and yet their expression is meaningful and necessary. It is a self-committal which clarifies the intention, strengthening and increasing it. Thus the prayers we utter clarify our spiritual longings, deepen our communion with God, and increase our sense of real and effective sharing in Jesus Christ's work of salvation among men. In the confession of our sins we clarify our inner conviction that we are sinful, we deepen our sense of sin and at the same time our longing for God's mercy, and we increase our watchfulness with regard to temptation and our knowledge of the love of Christ. We might apply to the practice of the confession of sins, which is at bottom a prayer, the words of St Paul: 'We know not what we should pray for as we ought: but the Spirit itself maketh intercession for us with groanings which cannot be uttered. And he that searcheth the hearts knoweth what is the mind of the

Spirit' (Rom. 8.26-7). In confession the Spirit comes to aid our weakness; even the most careful self-examination can never reveal to us the full extent and complexity of our sin. But what matters essentially is not so much to compile a complete and exhaustive list of our private faults, but, in respect of this or that major deficiency in our Christian obedience, to show ourselves for what we are and to present ourselves before God as beggars for his mercy. It is the action of the Holy Spirit which, in answer to our prayer, must show us our poverty and the confession of it that we must make; and then he that searcheth the hearts will know the sincere expression of our faults.

We may be convinced of the necessity of confessing our sins to God, but still hesitate to recognize the value of the presence of a witness of our confession. It is in the same context of self-committal in obedience to Christ that we should see the need of a confessor. A confession made in private to God, in the secrecy of one's private room, may be a means of evading the necessity of any real repentance. It is easy to admit one's sin to someone whom one knows to be fully aware of it already. There is also the fact that we too easily become accustomed to the idea of the presence and the holiness of God. The presence of a witness on behalf of God and of the Church makes more concrete for us the fact that God is there, that he is listening, grieving, and forgiving. The confessor, as a sign of the presence and the holiness of God, imparts to our confession a quality of committal and surrender which is an aid to humility. Furthermore, the presence of the confessor makes it possible for us to hear the liberating words of absolution.

Confession, then, as essentially a seeking after the mercy of Christ, prevents us from taking God's forgiveness for granted. Too often the absence of a habit of confession contributes to the idea that forgiveness is a natural function of God, and that we have some sort of right to it. Now, though we are to hope that God is greater than our heart and that if our heart condemn us, God who knows all things forgives us, we must not imagine that we need not repent and ask for forgiveness. Our peace of heart before God must not make us forget that he is just and that he grieves over our wrongdoing. 'If we confess our sins, he is faithful and just to forgive us our sins, and to cleanse us from all unrighteousness' (I John 1.9). Confession is a way of renewing in ourselves the certainty of the faithfulness and justice of God. The Lord is faithful to the promise which he made to his Apostles to remit the sins of those to whom the Church remits them. He is just in that he does not condemn us, knowing all the reasons for our weakness and our failures.

Whereas there are some who, through not practising confession, may be encouraged whether they admit it or not in the idea of automatic forgiveness by an indulgent God, there are some over-scrupulous people who in similar circumstances may become the victims of a guilt-complex. In the one case the absence of confession encourages facile optimism and a dangerous attitude of indifference to the gravity of sin; in the other it induces a tortured pessimism which leads to worried and neurotic introspection. The practice of confession makes possible the attainment of a balance in our spiritual life between a deep and lucid conviction of sin and an unshakeable and liberating certainty that God loves us. Thus we take seriously the holiness and justice of God—and therefore our sin as well, realizing at the same time that there are no fetters from which absolution will not deliver us. Confession thus nourishes the Christian life, giving us a deepening awareness of our sins and the temptations that beset us, and also an increasing joy in thankfulness to Christ, who endlessly pardons and blots out all our offences towards him.

Confession and absolution are in the Church the signs which renew our fellowship with Christ. Since to sin means to be unfaithful towards him, an infidelity which is the cause of the grief of his Passion and of the holy jealousy of Jehovah, it is meet and right that we should make this movement of reconciliation and peace towards him. Sin severs us not only from Christ, but also from the Church which is his Body. Our unfaithfulness to

75

Christ is also unfaithfulness to the Church. The confessor is the representative of both. We must be reconciled also with the Church which surrounds the Lord in heaven and is militant here on earth with us. So we renew our fellowship not only with the Lord, but also with all the saints who have gone before us and who rejoice in the forgiveness which God grants to us. 'There is joy in the presence of the angels of God over one sinner that repenteth' (Luke 15.10).

Confession of our sins does not bring us the assurance of pardon and consolation merely by reminding us of what Jesus Christ did once for all on the Cross for our sins. Faith is not a memory, even a vivid one, of the past; it is a firm assurance of the reality of the eternity—and so of the present reality—of the salvation and peace which are in Jesus Christ. 'If any man sin, we have an advocate with the Father, Jesus Christ the righteous: and he is the propitiation for our sins: and not for ours only, but also for the sins of the whole world' (I John 2.1-2). We have a present defender who pleads our cause, and he is the Lamb as it had been slain, the Victim of the Cross, resurrected and glorified. Jesus Christ makes a present reality for us of the mystery of his Passion, and in absolution we enter into the present reality of his eternal sacrifice. God's forgiveness, then, depends on the death and resurrection of Christ, accomplished once for all, but it is applied personally to us by the glorified Christ, through absolution. Our faith does not look backward into the past, but to the present reality of the salvation which Christ has won and is winning for us. The sacraments are the signs of this present reality. It is therefore not enough to say that Christ has won for us the mercy of God and reconciliation by his Passion, and that all we have to do is to believe in this salvation. This manner of thinking makes the Cross a reality of the past, and turns faith into a comforting memory. We must believe that everything was accomplished for our redemption in the historical person of Jesus, but that this same Jesus, resurrected and ascended, 'ever liveth to make intercession for us' (Heb. 7.25); that means that here and now he lets us share in his

76

life, and that in this intimate communion with him the benefits of his redemptive work are made available to us all. The sign of absolution requires of us faith in the 'It is finished' of the Cross, and opens our hearts to the love of Christ and to the lively assurance that he is interceding for us effectively now. The gift of God's forgiveness, which was made once and for all to the Church by Jesus Christ, must continually be meditated upon in faith in God's Word, and made our own through the effective sign of absolution.[1]

[1] See D. Bonhoeffer, *Life Together*, S.C.M. Press, London, 1954, pp. 100-12, the chapter on Confession and Communion. These few pages set before us in sincerity and truth the spiritual riches of the theology of confession, studied strictly in the light of the Gospel and of tradition.

CHAPTER FIVE

CONFESSION AND PSYCHOANALYSIS[1]

THE advent of psychological science and in particular of psycho-analysis raises serious problems for the Church, especially as regards confession and spiritual direction. There are some who think that psychoanalysis represents a considerable danger to Christian faith, that there is a risk that it may displace confession and spiritual direction, and so substitute in the minds of believers psychological notions and interpretations of certain religious phenomena for the actual dogma of the faith. Discoveries in the field of psychoanalysis are tending to provoke in the Church a theological and spiritual crisis comparable with that brought about by the great scientific discoveries of the end of the nineteenth century and the beginning of the twentieth. It can with truth be said that we have entered a psychological age in which the laws of a new and developing science are calling in question many accepted beliefs. The Roman Catholic Church is beginning to suspect a certain 'rivalry' between the practice of psychoanalysis and that of confession. The authorities of that Church have thought it wise to issue certain warnings.[2]

It is to be hoped that the consideration of the unfortunate effects of psychoanalysis on the faith of believers in certain cases will not lead to a hardening of the Church's attitude to that science. Christians must open their minds to the possibility of an intelligent synthesis of apparent contradictions and difficulties. After having thought that discoveries relating to anthropology and

[1] See E. Thurneysen, *op. cit.*, Ch. 10 and 11, 'Cure d'âme et psychologie' and 'Cure d'âme et psychothérapie', pp. 182-234.

[2] See the Pope's discourse on this subject in 1952, and his speech on 15 April 1953 to the Fifth International Congress of Psychotherapy and Clinical Psychology.

the age of the earth upset completely the doctrine of Creation, we have come to accept the assertions of science without denying the truth contained in the narratives of Genesis. No one today can claim with authority that scientific anthropology contradicts the biblical narrative of Creation, or that that narrative is not 'true' because it is not scientific in character. What happens is that science records objective facts and draws from them certain conclusions, upon which it bases explanatory hypotheses which in any case are always subject to revision. Genesis, on the other hand, makes no claim whatsoever to this scientific or historical objectivity, but, being God's revelation, it uses narratives from different literary traditions to transmit the doctrine of Creation, according to which God is the author of all things. This truth is addressed to the faith that is implanted by the Holy Ghost, and cannot in any respect contradict the discoveries and hypotheses of science so long as the science of which we are speaking does not overstep its proper limits. The difficulties often raised for the Church by science have arisen when the latter has not kept to the simple experience of facts and the pure working hypothesis, but has transformed itself into a more or less materialist philosophy. The difficulties sometimes raised for the scientist by Christian theology have arisen from a confusion between dogmatic truth, addressed to faith, which can thereupon reflect upon itself, and a so-called universal and natural truth on which faith might be constructed. Where this view was held, the calling in question of the early chapters of Genesis aroused the fear that the whole edifice of Christian faith would crumble. This was because of the placing on the same level of two different modes of knowledge, and the attribution to them of the same object. But it is not the function of science to prove the existence of God, while the sole function of theology is to affirm who he is and what he does.

These are two fields of investigation which do not overlap in any way; two modes of interpretation of creation which have different sources and different laws. *Mutatis mutandis*, it is as false to see a conflict between the scientific interpretation and the theological view of the world, as it is inconceivable that we should oppose this same scientific conception to the aesthetic perception of the universe. There is no more conflict between anthropological science and the Genesis stories than between the anatomical description of a face and its interpretation in a portrait.

The danger that some Christians believe they see in psychoanalysis is one which might be termed 'psychologism': by this I mean a one-sided interpretation of all psychological, spiritual, and moral phenomena in accordance with the norms established by analytical science. The theological consequences of this psychologism are likely to be a certain dogmatic relativism and a certain moral complacency. Such fears are not without foundation, and we must preserve an attitude of vigilant attention with regard to them. According to psychology, terms such as sin, repentance, faith, and love, as used in Christian thought, are an interpretation of phenomena which that science recognizes in its field of investigation only as psychological facts. Does not sin then tend to become merely a disease of the mind—serious perhaps, but one which may be cured by a proper course of treatment, or which must be accepted as an inevitable factor of our human nature? Some Christians see this psychoanalytical interpretation of sin as eliminating from the mind all idea of responsibility and all desire for repentance. If it is right that psychology should not take account of sin as an ontological reality, seeing in it only an interpretation made by the religious mind, the Christian is not for that reason obliged to limit himself to this restricted explanation of human misery. The Church recognizes, in fact, that sin—which is essentially a revolt against God, that is to say a lack of love for him and for what he has created—brings in its train a whole series of psychological and even physical consequences. Disease, either of mind or of body, is a more or less remote result of sin; if not of individual sin, at least of original or collective sin. Sin, therefore, produces a whole field of psychological results which may themselves be a proper sphere for psychoanalysis. Within its own limits, psychoanalysis, whether practised by a Christian or an agnostic, is not called upon to consider the theological or metaphysical causes of what we call sin.

The doctor who treats a disease is not, as a doctor, called upon to seek or indicate the particular spiritual or moral causes of the disease, but rather to heal it with the means which science puts at his disposal. The psychoanalyst limits himself to the discernment of the purely psychological causes of a state of disorder or neurosis. These causes may be for him either primary or secondary, according to whether he is agnostic or Christian, but in either case, in the exercise of his profession he is not required to seek further. This limitation of the domain of psychology, which is quite proper to it as a science, permits the Christian cure of the soul to be exercised alongside psychoanalysis, without competing or in any way being confused with it. Indeed, for the Church, it is not sufficient that a man be liberated from this or that complex; it is necessary also that absolution and spiritual direction should assure him of the divine forgiveness, without which he would be well but not sanctified, in a precarious condition spiritually and in danger of moral complacency. On the other hand it must be recognized that the psychoanalytical point of view has its uses in the effective exercise of the ministry of confession and direction. In fact, the substitution of a psychological explanation of what appears to be a sin makes it possible sometimes to rid the self-examination and the confession itself of considerations which have nothing to do, properly speaking, with the spiritual life.

The psychological analysis of sin, so far from weakening the Christian's sense of sin and responsibility, will in fact make him more acutely aware of these things. It is of the greatest importance that we should be able to discern what in us is sinful—and so ought to be repented of and confessed—and what is physiological or psychological in character. The latter may, like disease, be deplored as a consequence of general or individual sin, but it pertains rather to the domain of pathology than that of spiritual direction. It is important to emphasize once more that these considerations must not be allowed to whittle away human responsibility; but it is necessary to the proper exercise of the ministry of confession and direction that absolution and counsel should have as their object in the first place the state of sin, and not some pathological condition. It is not my wish to draw too absolute a line of demarcation between domains which are sometimes interdependent. Absolution and spiritual direction may have a healing effect which is not only spiritual but also psychological or physical; just as psychoanalytical treatment sometimes has repercussions in the realm of faith and charity. But such secondary and exceptional results must not lead us into a confusion between the practice of confession and that of psychoanalysis. It is right that the principles and the spheres of pastoral ministry and of psychological treatment should be clearly distinguished.

This basic distinction between the sin which is the concern of confession and direction, and the psychological weakness or the physical disease which are dealt with by analysis or by medicine, is made, I believe, by St Paul himself. In II Corinthians 12.7-10; 13.4 the Apostle expounds his teaching on weakness. He declares: 'Lest I should be exalted above measure through the abundance of the revelations, there was given to me a thorn in the flesh, the messenger of Satan to buffet me, lest I should be exalted above measure. For this thing I besought the Lord thrice, that it might depart from me. And he said unto me, My grace is sufficient for thee: for my strength is made perfect in weakness. Most gladly therefore will I rather glory in infirmities, in reproaches, in necessities, in persecutions, in distresses for Christ's sake: for when I am weak, then am I strong.' We cannot know what was the nature of the thorn in the flesh or the weaknesses which afflicted St Paul, whether they were physical or psychological. The important thing in this text is to notice that what the Apostle considers as a consequence of his pride is not sin, but a sort of painful goad which reminds him constantly of his human and sinful nature. His inner life and his mystical ecstasies might cause him to boast, but most fortunately the weakness of his nature brings him back to humility. The thorn in his flesh he also calls a messenger of Satan; that is to say that it is a manifestation of the sinfulness of his human nature, but it is not itself the sin of which he ought to repent. On the contrary, he considers that he ought to glory in his weaknesses, which are for him a means of proving that the strength which is manifest in his ministry is not a personal strength, but the power of Christ dwelling in him. Without this weakness, the Apostle might forget he is a sinner and believe, and lead others to believe, in a quite private power of his own, due to his saintliness; but he has in him the thorn, a messenger of Satan at his elbow to humble him. He had thought that he should be relieved of it in order the better to live his Christian life and perform his ministry; he had prayed, and the Lord had shown him that he must be content with his grace, and that his strength was made perfect in weakness. St Paul understood that like Christ 'crucified through weakness' yet living 'by the power of God', he and all 'we also are weak in him, but we shall live with him by the power of God'. Sickness or psychological trouble, so far from being a serious hindrance to our fellowship with Christ, may on the contrary associate us more closely with his Passion.

This means that it is not essential to the Christian life to find some sort of psychological equilibrium; it might on the contrary encourage a feeling of self-satisfaction fatal to faith. I believe, then, that psychoanalysis must remain as an indispensable treatment for those cases only which are really pathological. It is only in cases where Christian life and ministry are rendered impossible, where there is a complete blocking in the sanctification of the individual, and where all those around him suffer because of his disease, that one must advise a complete analysis. The Christian ought of course to be aware that holiness is not the same as equilibrium, but that the latter is only a necessary psychological condition making possible the former in particular cases where the ministry of confession and direction proves ineffective. The life of every Christian has its inner weaknesses, necessities, and distresses, and suffers injuries and persecutions from without; and he who prays to be delivered from them may receive the same answer as

St Paul. He must then strive to look upon his troubles as a goad urging him to be humble, a thorn opening his heart to a wider understanding of his fellow-men and a deeper charity, a means of closer fellowship with the crucified Christ. If he can accept his infirmities as the 'marks of Jesus' in his body, he will find peace and comfort in the Word of God, in the Sacrament, in confession, and in spiritual direction. But if these are of no avail to him, and his weaknesses are a constant source of backsliding, of lack of charity, and of the failure of the Church's ministrations to him, then he may consider having recourse to psychoanalysis.

There is a risk that an agnostic psychoanalysis may interpret the repentance indispensable to the practice of confession as a guilt-complex, and this is a real difficulty for the Church. Psychoanalysis is of course aimed at the liberation of the patient from complexes, and that of guilt may be considered as one of those which play a very great part in neuroses. But Christianity claims that repentance is a necessary element in the spiritual life; there can be no true confession or absolution without sincere repentance. Here again we must make certain distinctions which will show more clearly what confession is. Repentance is not regret that one is a man, subject to the difficulties inherent in a human nature troubled by the consequences of original sin. It is not concerned with the weakness or the thorn in the flesh that every man recognizes in himself. Its sole object is the sin voluntarily embraced by a self-centred and proud creature, greedy for independence. It is sincere contrition aroused by recognition of one's lack of love for God and men. It is essentially the painful realization of a rupture of communion with Jesus Christ. The guilt-complex, on the other hand, is a morbid feeling of being at fault in every action dictated by one's instincts. Behind the feeling of guilt there lies the idea that everything pertaining to our human nature, to our instincts, and to the world of created things, is bad. It is the result of a dualistic conception of human nature, according to which we are composed of an inferior corporeal nature, and a superior spiritual one. This conception is not Christian. The view of the Bible is that the whole of man is carnal, and each of the elements of which his nature is composed is subject both to sin and to sanctification. Christian theology believes in the corruption of the spirit, and confesses the resurrection of the flesh—that is to say of the whole being which is in bondage to sin—hence of the body as well.

Very often spiritual direction encounters, in place of real repentance of sin, a guilt-complex which represents a refusal to accept a humanity subject to weakness. It is here that a knowledge of psychoanalysis can be of great help. It is in fact one more of the ruses of Satan, disguised as an angel of light, to plunge the Christian into blank despair over his human nature. One of the ways the Devil uses saints is to implant a guilt-complex in them. As for repentance, it presupposes hope. It is the condition of absolution, a step towards inner peace. The morbid feeling of guilt is the opposite of what we saw to exist in the mind of St Paul. He rejoiced in weaknesses and exulted in them—that is to say that he fully accepted his humanity. God sets before us the example of Christ crucified in weakness and requires us to be content with his grace and with his strength working in us, in spite of our miserable state. So we are not to bewail our human nature with its limitations, but to repent of our complaisance towards the temptations which it sets before us. We must accept our humanity, our nature, our instincts, our sexuality, and place them at the service of the love of Christ. To shrink away from our humanity could only aggravate the possibilities of temptation, and would do nothing towards gaining true liberty in the spiritual life. Confusion between true repentance of sin and a guilt-complex regarding nature can cause serious disorders in a Christian's life. How many there are, badly directed and not in the habit of confession, who have a guilt-complex about sex, for instance, and have had their lives poisoned by it! Often they have unconsciously imagined prohibitions where there were none, and their complex has forced them into an attitude of servility, which has prevented them from giving themselves generously to a love willed by God. Often confession and spiritual direction uncover cases of suffering where a person has turned in upon himself in this way, and can effect liberation from the guilt-complex and lead the sufferer to real repentance. André Gide on several occasions fought against this feeling of guilt, which he found in a certain Protestant society. His analysis, often made with great insight, does not, unfortunately, lead to true repentance, but has often been used as the justification of a certain libertinism. We may however retain his critique of Protestant moralism. In Alissa, in *La porte étroite*, do we not find the same sexual guilt-complex as is met with in some badly-directed Christians? Sex and human love are looked upon as the worst kind of sin, unavoidable though they be. Alissa feels herself called upon to make the renunciation which is an unconscious symbol of her refusal to accept a legitimate love. The 'narrow door' through which she passes is that of her sexual complex, and not that of true repentance of her sin, or of positive committal in complete self-giving to the love of Christ alone. Psychoanalysis, which has shown us the importance of sex in the whole of man's psychological make-up, has by the same token put us on guard against a conviction of sin that always bears upon our sexual desires. Confession and spiritual direction ought to make possible the attainment of a balanced view of our sinfulness, reminding us that the greatest sin is lack of love for God and for our fellow-men. All other sins flow from that one. How is it that Christians pay so much attention to their sexual difficulties and are so careless about their attitude to their fellows, if it is not because their psychological make-up is influencing their spiritual life? While psychoanalysis must assert the primacy of sex in man's psychological make-up, spiritual direction must not allow itself to be unduly influenced, and while recognizing the great importance of this problem for the inner life, it must at the same time bring to notice all the forms of sin other than sexual disorder, and bring men's consciences back always to the question of sacrificial and self-giving love.

Some Christians suspect psychoanalytical science of interpreting faith as a phenomenon of unconscious projection, on the level of myth, of childhood experiences. Thus the fatherhood of God, the expiatory and substitutive death of the Son of God our brother, the Virgin Birth, and many other tenets of the Christian faith, would be in grave danger of receiving a purely psychological interpretation. Though we must categorically reject the assimilation of the history of our salvation to a psychological myth, and the interpretation of Christian dogma as symbols of the collective unconscious, we may admit that certain theological interpretations and religious attitudes are not without some unconscious psychological motivation. Without in any way detracting from the genuineness of certain authentic theological positions, it is possible to detect a psychological kinship between this or that orthodox or liberal doctrinal position and a particular psychological temperament. A Christian's personal faith may stress a particular aspect of revelation according to his own religious temperament. One, with a headstrong and active character, will emphasize the role of the believer as a collaborator with God in his work of salvation; another, on the other hand, more emotional and passive, will insist on the omnipotence and unique effectiveness of grace. In cases where the believers concerned are conscious of their temperaments, and desire through spiritual self-discipline to counteract their effects, their attitudes will be the inverse of what I have just described. The effects of the psychology of the Christians concerned can be seen in many forms of public worship or of private devotion. The realization of this interdependence of the spiritual and the psychological spheres must not, however, lead us to look upon the truths and doctrines of the Christian faith as being only relative. It is only personal interpretations or schools of theology, or modes of religious expression, that are affected. The fact that the faith of a Christian is often stamped with the mark of his psychological temperament need not make us doubt its basic objectivity or its transcendental origin. Rather should it reveal to us—and make us wonder at it—the infinite richness of Christian truth which allows every human type to express in his own way the mystery of salvation. The psychological interpretation of faith is an invitation to intellectual humility in the theologian, and a proof of the catholicity of Christian dogma, which answers the universal aspirations of men of all times and places, and which takes possession of the whole of their being, spirit, mind, and body.

For the Christian, love sums up all God's commandments. Being a Christian means essentially loving God and loving one's neighbour. These two commandments are alike. It is a fact that true Christianity rejects both the pure contemplation of God for his own sake and mere activist philanthropy. Christian love is an unreserved attachment to Christ, in whom God and man are united in one and the same Person. In Christ it sees the perfect man, the man who must be loved selflessly, in utter forgetfulness of self and readiness for sacrifice even unto death. Christian love is also directed towards man, but not for his own sake. In our neighbour it recognizes the face of Jesus Christ. So love of God and love of man are fused into a single love of Christ, God and man. But not only is love the new commandment of the Gospel, it is also the very nature of God: God is love. It is because God first loved us that we can love him and each other. This means that Christian love is different from ordinary human love. It is modelled on that of God himself. 'In this was manifested the love of God towards us, because that God sent his only begotten Son into the world, that we might live through him. Herein is love, not that we loved God, but that he loved us, and sent his Son to be the propitiation for our sins' (I John 4.9-10). It is of the nature of Christian love, then, to act without expecting anything in return. Christian love makes the first move, the Christian takes the initiative without waiting for a sign from his neighbour. And in his love the Christian gives of his best, as God gave his only Son. He gives, as it were, himself, sacrifices, renounces, and forgets himself in union with Christ who is the propitiation for our sins. Finally, Christian love desires that others should live, as God wills that we should have life through Christ. It seeks for man that true joy and happiness which the Gospel calls his salvation.

That is why it is repugnant to the Church to see (as is the case with certain agnostic psychoanalysts) Christian love considered as a sort of sublimation of human love. Indeed, none of the characteristics of love as I have defined it supports the idea of a sublimation of that kind. The Gospel states that love comes from on high; it is modelled on God's love for man. Though this is the dogmatic definition of love which the Gospel gives, its practice in our sinful human life is less pure than the ideal which is thus set before every Christian. Our love for God and for our neighbour, though it is a creation in us of the Holy Spirit, makes use of our human nature. It is the part of spiritual discipline or of abstinence, the practice of renunciation and sacrifice, to help us to distinguish between real Christian love and the mere sublimation of human affection. Nevertheless it ought not to be thought that Christian love in all its purity and simplicity is always a possibility. There is nothing in suffering humanity more widespread than this lack of love and the deep-seated emotional complexes to which it may give rise. It is rare that a child has ever been loved as much as he wanted to be, and adults frequently have to suffer the desertion complex which has its origin in this unsatisfied thirst for love. That the believer who encounters Christ finds that the love of God and of his brethren in the Church goes some way to satisfy his unfulfilled emotional tendencies, does not mean that his attachment to Christ and to his fellow-men is a mere unconscious transfer. It is indeed the pure first-given sacrificial love of Jesus Christ at work in him and dictating his behaviour, but it is made incarnate in his sinful creaturely flesh, using his human nature. We cannot but wonder at the depth of the love of God, which does not spring from the heart of man, but is the pure gift of grace, yet takes possession of our whole being with all its weaknesses, its aspirations, its disappointments, its lack of love and its thirst for it, and fills our hearts to overflowing with generosity towards men.

Analysis may be of salutary help in putting the spiritual director on his guard against those frequent cases of confusion between a religious call and a simple affective transfer or the sublimation of disappointed human love. The classic example of the girl who enters a convent after a disappointment in love is more than a romantic myth. Such psychological situations are of course not always simple, nor are they always conscious or admitted. There are some who have felt themselves capable of experiencing only one real love, and where this first love has proved itself a failure their fidelity to it prevents them from giving themselves to any other. A woman whose first experience of sex has been a shock to her may revolt against marriage and wreck every attempt she makes. A Christian vocation, or total commitment to the religious life, may in such a case awaken a response apparently dictated purely by the Holy Spirit. There would be no spiritual advantage to be gained from leaving a Christian in ignorance of the human motives which might lie behind one aspect of his response to God's call; on the contrary, if he committed himself in ignorance of the motives behind his vocation he would be running the risk of exposing himself at some future time to the gravest spiritual crises. Of course the strength of the commitment or of the monastic vow may very well be greatly fortified through the experience of a crisis of this sort, but it would perhaps be better to avoid such a crisis by first submitting to an honest self-examination. The discovery by a spiritual director who is alive to the uses of psychoanalysis, of emotional motives underlying a person's engagement in a particular task within the Church, may well lead him to advise its renunciation, because of the trouble which these unsurmountable human elements may cause. For example, a woman who discovers that her emotional troubles are due to a homosexual tendency may be advised not to choose a task in education to which she perhaps feels called with all her being. For her to be among girls to whom she would in spite of herself be incapable of giving a balanced view of marriage could well be harmful. While this may be true of individual cases, it would be wrong to generalize. What I have said about the love of God, and of the desire for complete dedication which takes hold of our whole being, may lead the spiritual director to conclude that a vocation, which when considered in the light of psychoanalysis seems to be a dangerous sublimation, is in fact the fruit of God-given love for Christ and for men which may go on growing in purity. The transfer of an unsatisfied love to God made Man, in prayer and worship, and to our fellow-men, in mutual service and sacrifice, may be the means which God has chosen by which to make incarnate his pure love in our hearts.

People who have suffered emotional injury may sometimes cling to an eschatological hope for the end of the world and the Second Coming of Christ and the establishment of the Kingdom of God. This is because they see in the fulfilment of their hope an end to their suffering and the possibility of consolation, retribution, and the rediscovery of the love they have lost. Once again, this in no way invalidates the authenticity of their hope: God who used our flesh to reveal himself to us, Christ who was crucified in our weakness, wills to use our humanity and to be glorified through the thorns in our human flesh. So the inter-penetration of our emotional tendencies and the pure love of Christ for us, which gives birth in us to disinterested love for God and for our fellows, so far from giving us cause to doubt the authenticity of our vocation, ought rather to make us apprehend with St Paul what is the breadth, and length, the depth and height of the love of Christ, and to know this love which passes all knowledge, that we may be filled with all the fulness of God (Eph. 3.18-19). The risk the Christian runs is not that God may make his supernatural love incarnate in his powers of natural love, but that he may ignore his own often disordered emotional tendencies, and that he may not face frankly his own sinfulness, and be quite honest about his weaknesses and the thorns in his flesh, when seeking the help of a confessor, a spiritual director, or a Christian friend.

It is not absolutely necessary to be psychoanalysed in order to rid oneself of harmful emotional complexes and attain the equilibrium which would permit of a pure Christian love. In fact such equilibrium and purity can never be attained by the sinner. He must accept the constant tension between his nature and grace, between his passions and the sacrifice which Christian love requires of him. He must even bear in mind that this inner struggle can become a source of charity, and make him more sensitive and understanding towards the sufferings of others. In this tension between his mastered passions and the charity of Christ, he comes to know more truly the love of God for us which was revealed in Jesus; that is to say that he experiences the Cross, accepting self-sacrifice for the joy of his fellows. There is no greater love than this, that a man should lay down his life for his friends (John 15.13). It is true that in certain cases of neurosis psychoanalysis may help towards the realization of a Christian vocation. But here again there are some Christian psychoanalysts who hold that a vocation followed in full recognition of the neurosis on which it is partly based may still bear rich fruit in obedience to firm direction. One Christian psychoanalyst has asserted to me that a monastic vocation may give rise to a neurotic state due to the limitations of liturgical and community life, and the demands it makes for sustained obedience and spiritual direction. The succour and the strength to be found in the Church and in a community may do much to help a man to maintain himself in obedience to Christ, in spite of a thorn in his flesh—even a serious and painful one. He experiences there the truth of the fact that the strength of God is made perfect in weakness (II Cor. 12.9).

Obedience, and the readiness to be directed which is its fruit, have always been looked upon in the Church as the test of a profound spiritual life. True Christian obedience has as its object the Person of God himself and his will as expressed in his Word. God reveals himself to us through the instruments which he himself has instituted and which constitute the Church, the Body of Christ. There is a false spirituality which envisages obedience as addressing itself to God without any intermediary. This leads to angelism, and leaves the Christian helpless. The problem raised by this attitude is in fact a false one. It is true that Christ is the only mediator and advocate, and that he alone has a right to our complete obedience. But it was the will of Christ himself to leave us a sign of his royal authority, as well as of his unique priesthood and his prophetic mission. That sign is his mystic Body, the Church, exercising her ministry through men empowered and ordained for that purpose. The Church and the ministry are to be seen not as intermediaries, but as signs revealing and realizing the sole authority of Christ. For the Christian, then, obedience cannot be purely 'spiritual' and individual: it is made incarnate and concrete in obedience to the Church and her ministry. In order that the sole and absolute authority of Jesus Christ may always be clearly signified by the authority of the Church and her ministers, the latter must never be considered as having personal rights and powers. They are but instruments and practical, though necessary, signs of the exercise of the divine authority. True Christian obedience will be revealed in simple respect for, and readiness to act under the direction of, those to whom the ministry of authority has been entrusted; but it will beware of the attitude of servility and hero-worship which might give rise to confusion between the authority of God and human authority, between spiritual obedience and slavish submission. The obedience of the Gospel does not weaken the personality, but on the contrary develops it through renunciation of self-will and increasing awareness of fellowship in a community. The Christian who has learnt obedience, instead of remaining shut up within the bounds of his own individualism, forges this egoism through contact with his fellows, learns to put himself in another's place, to look upon himself as being that other. Instead of being limited to a single personality of his own, he is enriched by that of his neighbour. Christ's commandment does not oblige the Christian to love others while ignoring himself and repressing his own personality. The Saviour said: 'Thou shalt love thy neighbour as thyself' (Matt. 22.39). So the Christian must love his neighbour as if his neighbour were himself; he must know how to put himself in the place of others, to love them as he is tempted to love himself. This command, then, does not annihilate the person, but universalizes it, and develops it in a way that no psychological advice or moral exhortation could ever do.

Christian obedience is sometimes interpreted as the expression of an inferiority complex. We have just seen what its real meaning is, and that it is in no way obsessional or degrading to the human personality. Nevertheless, it must be recognized that obedience may be expressed in certain ways that may justify criticism on the part of psychological analysis. Obedience may in fact sometimes be a spiritual expression of infantilism. There are some personalities, repressed in childhood or not properly prepared for the responsibilities of adult life, which remain at an infantile or adolescent stage of development. They are then in danger of reproducing in their obedience the attitude of the child towards his father. This attitude, of course, is often ambivalent in its nature, so that the individual passes from slavish admiration of a spiritual director to the most violent rebellion against his authority. One may wonder whether certain religious rules of life do not tend to perpetuate this infantile psychology. This could be the case, for instance, with the Rule of St Benedict, in which authority is firmly based on a patriarchal and paternalist social system. A naïve infantilism of this sort is a well-known failing among monks, where it is the fruit of an obedience not always sufficiently enlightened by the teaching of the Gospel. Psychoanalysis is often justified in pointing out these distorted expressions of Christian obedience, and may help to recall a man to a more virile and fully conscious adult attitude. It is not required of the Christian that he should remain a child all his life. Christ does indeed tell us to become as little children, but he is speaking of the humility and simplicity of a childlikeness far removed from infantilism. As St Paul declares: 'When I was a child I spake as a child . . . : but when I became a man, I put away childish things' (I Cor. 13.11). So one must put away one's childish psychology in order to reach adulthood; then one must, through obedience and humility, become 'as' a child—that is to say, return to the purity of heart and the trusting attitude of the child. Humility is a hard-won victory for the adult man, not an hypocritical naïvety. In any case, it is not an end in itself, but a means of attaining joy, peace, and resurrection. Christ requires us to lose our life, but this is in order to find it. The aim of Christian humility is a quite special intimacy with the humiliated and crucified Jesus, in order to share in his glory.

Psychologists have sometimes seen in Christian abstinence a negative attitude of satisfaction in suffering for its own sake. There is no doubt that some ascetic practices reveal a sort of masochism which is the consequence of a neurotic state. Numerous cases of this could be quoted from the history of the Church. Neurosis certainly plays its part in the ascetic zeal of one such as St Marie Marguerite Alacoque, for example. As I have already said, we must be persuaded that it is God's will to use these psychological complexes in order to reveal himself through the heroism of a saint. The fact that a masochistic tendency is discernible in one of the heroes of the faith does nothing to devalue the saintliness of a Christian who is seeking to express with the means at his disposal his participation in the sufferings of Christ. The fact that a psychoanalyst may have diagnosed a castration complex in an ascetic does not mean that his humility and holiness are thereby diminished, so long as these psychological or neurotic circumstances do not prevent him from living faithfully in charity according to the Gospel. There are certain types of neurotic asceticism in which suffering and misery are cultivated for their own sakes, and in these cases analysis may help towards an equilibrium in Christian obedience more in conformity with the Gospel. Nevertheless the search for equilibrium must be undertaken with great prudence, for it would be disastrous if a psychological analysis were to take away from a Christian all inclination for spiritual discipline, and were to turn a saint into a healthy animal. When we read the life of St Francis of Assisi, so sane and balanced in most respects, but certainly in others possessed of an exaggerated inclination towards asceticism, we cannot help being glad that, with all its complexes, that great life was lived. What would be the result of psychoanalysing a Francis of Assisi?

95

Though Christian asceticism sometimes grows on psychological ground which favours excesses, its principles are free of any taint of masochism. It is not primarily a seeking after suffering, but a positive acceptance of it. The ministry of healing exercised by the Church clearly demonstrates that Christian faith will not countenance resignation in the face of physical or psychological disease.[1] By prayer, the laying on of hands, and anointing with oil, the Church fights supernaturally and positively against suffering. A Christian may be asked, as St Paul was, to accept a thorn in the flesh. We have already seen how the believer must accept such a weakness. Christian asceticism is essentially a discipline of the inner life, a discipline of prayer, of spiritual and moral life, which may imply some bodily exercise such as fasting. St Paul compares asceticism with a sport. It is not at all a matter of using ascetic practices in order to achieve more concentrated meditation, more detached from this world, despising one's body or attenuating one's psychological personality. Christian asceticism is not, of its nature, a system of bodily or mental exercises; it is only a physical and psychological form of prayer and self-giving. Like prayer, its aim is not the beatitude of the self in Nirvana, but the fulfilment of intercession and the resurrection of the body. 'Know ye not,' writes St Paul, 'that they which run in a race run all, but one receiveth the prize? So run, that ye may obtain' (I Cor. 9.24). Christian asceticism is a contest to gain an incorruptible crown. In the race which is set before the Christian, he must not run a zig-zag course, but straight to the goal. The Christian life implies discipline and sacrifice, in order more quickly to attain inner liberty. Asceticism is therefore a positive discipline, an effort which demands a man's whole energy. Using the language of the boxing-ring, St Paul describes asceticism thus: 'So fight I, not as one that beateth the air, but I keep under my body, and bring it into subjection: lest that by any means, when I have

[1] See B. Martin, *Le ministère de la guérison dans l'Eglise*, Labor et Fides, Geneva, 1952, p. 144. This book includes a useful discussion on the definition of a sacrament, in connection with the laying on of hands and anointing with oil. What it has to say could be applied to absolution; see pp. 126-36.

preached to others, I myself should be a castaway' (I Cor. 9.26-7).[1]
So when the Christian imposes all kinds of abstinences upon himself, it is not in order to annihilate his body and liberate his mind,
but, as in the case of the athlete, the better to run and the better to
fight, in order to be stronger in body and mind, and in order that
his whole being, mind, soul, and body, may in the end win the
incorruptible crown: the resurrection of the body and eternal life.

I have recognized the usefulness of psychoanalysis in certain
cases where the religious life suffers too great a handicap in the
form of complexes or neurosis. The advantage gained by this
psychological approach to the problems of the Christian life is
likely to be the purification of faith and piety, which often have an
admixture of natural religiosity or even of emotionalism. Moreover,
analysis, which reminds us of the primacy of the sexual element in
the psychological make-up, warns the Christian against giving a
false position to this element in the spiritual and moral sphere
also. Thanks to psychology, man is led to recognize, in accordance
with the Gospel, that sin is not sexuality, but lack of love for
Christ and for his fellow-men. Psychoanalysis and its consequences
in the spiritual realm often result in real moral liberation. We have
seen also the dangers of the psychological approach to the spiritual
life, the danger of reducing everything, even the most essential
dogma, to a matter of psychology: psychologism. The consequence of this deviation from faith may be, on the spiritual plane,
a dogmatic relativism which tends to turn the history of our
salvation into a series of myths, expressions of the collective
unconscious. On the moral plane the consequence may take the
form of a complacency which excuses everything, not out of
charity, but as a concession to our nature.

The true ministry of confession need not fear competition from
psychoanalysis, since while recognizing the limited role of the
latter, it acts on a supernatural level. Indeed, confession is not

[1] J. B. Phillips' translation of this passage is expressive: 'I am no
shadow-boxer, I really fight! I am my body's sternest master, for fear
that when I have preached to others, I should myself be disqualified'
(*Letters to Young Churches*, Geoffrey Bles, London, 1947, p. 52). *Tr.*

primarily a psychological release, but essentially a seeking for God's forgiveness, granted to man's sinful nature, and an awaiting of the absolution which confers the assurance of his mercy. The sacramental acts of confession and absolution are therefore always necessary to the full development of the inner life, even in the case of a person fully 'liberated' by psychoanalysis. Psychoanalysis may make it possible for a man to accept his humanity, but it does not follow that he no longer needs to repent the sinful consequences of that humanity. Humbling oneself, repenting, and confessing are positive acts whose aim is liberation, and not a conviction of despair over the impotence of our human nature. They are part of the complete and definitive liberation of the person which is signified by absolution. Though psychoanalysis may bring about a psychological and moral liberation, it remains a human liberty and holds no promise for a man so long as he has not understood by faith the mercy of God which Christ won for us once for all, and which is made real and present for us personally by sacramental absolution. There is between analysis and confession all the difference that exists between the psychological and the ontological. This distinction is perhaps more difficult to make as regards the relationship between analysis and spiritual direction. The latter does in fact show many more human and subjective characteristics than does sacramental confession, but it must be remembered that the points of view and the levels upon which each acts are different, that they are two complementary interpretations: the psychological judgement and the judgement of faith.

Although it is an advantage for the confessor, and particularly the director, to have some knowledge of psychoanalytical science, they ought not to practise psychoanalysis. The spheres must remain distinct, for their confusion would be harmful to both faith and science. The spiritual director who knows something of psychological problems will be able to discern the existence of a complex, but he must not let himself play the part of the psychoanalyst. If he judges that a neurotic state is an obstacle to spiritual life, he must advise the person concerned to consult a psychoanalyst. He himself acts only on the spiritual level of sacramental confession and the cure of souls. He must speak the language of the Gospel, of faith and of Christian obedience—not that of psychology. It is of course difficult in the course of a pastoral interview for the spiritual director to avoid entirely the use of the language of psychology. It all depends on the general tone of the direction he is giving. A chance remark of a psychological nature is not going to cause fatal confusion, so long as the Christian is always brought back to the consideration of his sin and urged to repent, and that the act of faith, brotherly love, obedience and spiritual discipline are enjoined upon him. If it is right that the confessor or director, although instructed in psychology—and even with advantage psychoanalysed themselves —should avoid all practice of analysis as such, the converse is equally important, in order always to preserve the purity and efficacy of these two complementary and different ministries. The Christian psychologist will always remember that, as a psychologist, he does not exercise the ministry of reconciliation. It would be wrong for him to arrogate to himself the rights of an accredited confessor, on the excuse that people come more readily to unburden themselves to him than to the pastor. They may prefer to do so because it is easier—it is often more 'comfortable' to have one's sin thought of as a weakness or even as a disease. A Christian psychologist who countenanced the confusion of sacramental confession with psychological release, of spiritual direction and prescriptions for good health, would be rendering the worst possible service both to the Church and to his own profession. What the Christian psychologist ought to do, when he has accomplished his task, is to direct his Christian patients towards the spiritual ministry of the Church.[1]

[1] On the relationship between psychology and the cure of souls, the following will be read with great profit: R. S. Lee, *Freud and Christianity*, J. Clarke, London, 1948; T. Bovet, *Lebendige Seelsorge*, P. Haupt, Berne, 1952; *Psychologie moderne et réflexion chrétienne*, A. Fayard, Paris, 1953. The last work contains several important contributions by Christian psychotherapists: in particular those by Drs Durand and Nodet, pp. 143-9 and 173-86.

CHAPTER SIX

THE CONFESSOR

CONFESSION is a proper part of the Church's ministry, and should be exercised habitually by every pastor. Some may have the particular gifts required for spiritual direction, but all are called to exercise the ministry of the confessor, just as all are called upon to baptize, to celebrate the Lord's Supper and all the sacramental acts. Thus the usual minister of confession is the consecrated pastor. We have already seen that this was Calvin's view when he wrote: '. . . since the Pastors must be considered more proper for [confession] than others, we ought chiefly to make choice of them. I say that they are more suitable than others, since, in their very vocation to the ministry, they are designated by God, to instruct us to subdue and correct our sins, and to certify us of God's goodness, for our consolation. For though the office of mutual admonition is committed to all Christians, yet it is especially confided to ministers. And so, while we all ought mutually to console each other, yet we see that ministers are constituted by God witnesses and as it were sureties, to certify our consciences of the remission of sins; insomuch that they themselves are said to remit sins and to loose souls.' Thus the pastor, as the minister of confession, has authority effectively to announce the pardon and absolution of God in the name of the Christian community, the universal Church. There is no question of his having a personal power in virtue of his ordination, or a greater moral and spiritual dignity. He has had delegated to him the unique power of forgiveness which belongs to Jesus Christ and which he entrusts to his Church, which speaks through her ministers. The ministry of spiritual direction is of quite a different character, and involves gifts of discernment not required by the ministry of confession.

It is important to define the authority of the minister in

confession. It is, in the first place, no different from the authority
of the ministry in general. The Apostle writes in the Epistle to the
Hebrews: 'Obey them that have the rule over you, and submit
yourselves: for they watch for your souls, as they that must give
account, that they may do it with joy, and not with grief: for that
is unprofitable for you' (Heb. 13.17). The obedience of which this
text speaks relates to the authority conferred by an ecclesiastical
function. It is because it is the duty of spiritual rulers to watch
over the salvation of souls, of which they will have to render
account, that we must obey them and even submit ourselves to
them. The authority of the confessor and the spiritual director
resides in the fact that they represent the community of the
Church. They represent it in virtue of their ordination; they are
the present and concrete expression of the authority of Jesus Christ
who alone possess the power to forgive. This ecclesiastic authority
forms part of the sacrament of which it is the living expression. It
is not to be confused with spiritual authority, which is, of course,
greatly to be desired as rendering the ministry more profound and
the direction more discerning and effective. Sacramental confession and absolution derive their efficacy only from Christ, who
confers ecclesiastic authority upon his ministers. An objection
commonly made concerning confession is that those who hear it
are no better than other people. That is the truth, but not an
objection. It is quite clear that the confessor does not presume upon
his personal spiritual authority or the exemplary character of his
life in order to have the right to exercise his ministry. If the
authority and efficacy of the ministry of reconciliation repose upon
the quality of the minister's personal religious life, it can neither
be exercised nor bear fruit—for who will dare to set himself up
as an example to others? If we are to have a full assurance of the
forgiveness of God in absolution, it is essential that the sole
authority of Jesus Christ be recognized in the ministry of the
confessor. If in addition he is imbued with great spiritual authority,
this fact will not give greater validity or effectiveness to the
sacrament, but it will demonstrate that the Gospel of which he is

the minister bears fruit in his own life, and thus provide one more reason for the faithful to confide in him. The faithful, however, cannot insist upon his having this spiritual authority: it is sufficient for them that their pastor is ordained by the Church, that he is clothed with the Church's authority, which is the sign of the presence of Christ's authority, to proclaim to them God's mercy and to loose their souls. To insist upon personal spiritual authority would be one more way of providing oneself with an excuse for avoiding confession. The pastor, for his part, who would then be straining after the acquisition of such spiritual authority, would in fact be tempted to sin, since it is not possible to desire that authority without something of spiritual pride. This is the case in the instance quoted by the Apostle of the ruler who exercises his ministry 'with grief', and is to the advantage of no one. Further, to require this spiritual authority as the basis of the ministry of confession is to fall back into a form of the theology of works, since it means that one makes the grace of God dependent upon human spirituality and morality. The teaching of the Gospel concerning grace implies a sacramental theology of the ministry, and therefore of confession, in which the whole emphasis must be laid on the objective and gratuitous nature of God's acts performed through the Church and the men who serve her. To obey and submit to our spiritual rulers solely because they have been given the duty of vigilance is to affirm that we believe in the unique action of grace and not in the merit or effectiveness of any human attitude or example. It also means giving back its joy and liberty to the ministry, since the pastor will no longer be straining after the acquisition of authority, but simply seeking to be obedient to Jesus Christ like any other Christian, without feeling that this is a necessary condition of the efficacy of his ministry. The pastor is not required to be sanctified differently from other Christians in order for his preaching or the Church's sacraments to be effective. In the matter of sanctification he is like any other faithful member of the Church. He will the more easily and freely be able to be so if the authority of his ministry is faithfully recognized. This Gospel doctrine of the Christian ministry, which insists on the objectivity of Christ's authority in the pastor, far from encouraging clericalism, on the contrary replaces the minister among the ranks of ordinary Christians, if not in regard to his particular function, at least in his life as a man and a Christian. What creates a gulf between the pastorate and the laity is the laying of too much stress on a need for spiritual authority in the former. The objective authority of his ordination simply confers upon the minister a particular charge, while permitting him to remain in men's minds a Christian like any other, just as his training and his degree give the doctor a particular responsibility and function without removing him from common humanity. This is a point especially well worth remembering in regard to the ministry of confession, in which the pastor must show himself fully human, although invested with the authority of Christ and with his power of absolution.

Belief in this sacramental authority, which alone is indispensable for the proper exercise of the ministry of confession, and the fact that the confessor and the director need not seek to acquire personal spiritual authority in order to make their ministry valid and effective, can be a spiritual danger for the pastor. Faced with the difficulties of the Christian life, he may tend to presume too much upon his position as a pastor. He falls then into the error of authoritarianism, which is fatal to his ministry. While the quality of the pastor's Christian life is not the basis of his ministry, the authority of which reposes solely in the promise of Jesus Christ, he must still be a good Christian among others. If he wants his flock to share in the divine treasure of which he is the dispenser, let him show in himself the fruits that treasure bears. If the practice of confession is to be encouraged, it is vital that the confessor should be a person of holy life. The pastor will therefore endeavour to be the first to avail himself of confession, through the practice of which he will learn humility and renunciation. It is not possible to be a true confessor or spiritual director if one does not oneself habitually practise confession and if one does not receive spiritual direction. It is not enough to talk and lecture on the subject of confession if we want to encourage its practice in the Church. Pastors must resolutely enter its discipline if they wish to see it desired by their flocks. In their own practice of confession they will seek especially the mortification of their tendencies towards authoritarianism over men's souls, jealousy of the ministry of others, and the spiritual pride which is the besetting sin of their office.

St Paul writes to Timothy: 'Let no man despise thy youth; but be thou an example of the believers, in word, in manner of life, in charity, in spirit, in faith, in purity. . . . Neglect not the gift that is in thee, which was given thee by prophecy, with the laying on of the hands of the presbytery. Meditate upon these things; give thyself wholly to them; that thy profiting may appear to all. Take heed unto thyself, and unto thy teaching. Continue in them: for in doing this thou shalt both save thyself, and them that hear thee' (I Tim. 4.12-16). The Apostle is exhorting Timothy to remember the authority with which he is invested, in spite of his youth, which the Church ought to respect. He has received it in his ordination, and on this fact his ministry rests. But what would be the use of the office and authority which make his ministry valid and efficacious in itself, if the faithful were not attracted to the practice of the Christian life through seeing the fruits of his spiritual life? They must, it is true, accept the fact of his ministry, but they may be stimulated if he himself endeavours to be 'an example of the believers'. His perseverance in the Christian life will save him himself, and will make it possible for the faithful to listen to him and to be saved also by his word, which is the vehicle of the Word of God.

St Paul wants the authority of this young man to be recognized in virtue of his ordination, but he warns him at the same time against misuse of that authority, reminding him that, a believer among believers, he must work out his own salvation. In doing so he puts Timothy on his guard against authoritarianism and pride. So great a temptation is this to the pastor, that Jesus himself warned us against it. Speaking of the scribes and Pharisees who sit in Moses' seat, he enjoins the people to do and observe all they say. 'But,' he adds, 'do not ye after their works: for they say, and do not. For they bind heavy burdens and lay them on men's shoulders; but they themselves will not move them with one of their fingers. But all their works they do for to be seen of men: they make broad their phylacteries, and enlarge the borders of their garments, and love the uppermost rooms at feasts, and the chief seats in the synagogues, and greetings in the markets, and to be called of men, Rabbi, Rabbi' (Matt. 23.1-7). Jesus casts no doubt upon the essential authority of the Word of God transmitted by the scribes and Pharisees. The fundamental authority of the ministry, of the confessor and of the director, reposes upon the facts of the preaching of God's Word and of ordination to represent the Church. The scribes and Pharisees are to be listened to in spite of their failings, because they expound Scripture and sit in Moses' seat. 'He that heareth you heareth me,' said Christ elsewhere (Luke 10.16), speaking this time to his apostles, and through them to the Church and her ministers. But though the Scribes and Pharisees have the authority necessary to the ministry because they occupy Moses' seat, they say and do not, to their condemnation. Jesus speaks first of the heavy burdens which the pastor may be tempted to lay on men's shoulders. The confessor and the director know what are the commandments of the Gospel, and they run the risk, in the name of these commandments, of not being sufficiently human to understand men's difficulties and to bring them progressively and without undue haste to a better obedience. It is at this point that their own experience of sin and forgiveness can inspire in them a greater compassion and gentleness of heart. Then Jesus deals with the problem of the spiritual pride of the director who, instead of the Word of God, holds up before the believer his own spiritual experience. And the great danger here is that he will be readier to reveal the positive side than the negative, and so to appear better in the eyes of the believer than he really is, with the result that the believer is discouraged.

Then Christ castigates false manifestations of authority. It is of course a good thing that there should be order in the Church; but those who have the ministry of authority must beware of loving to take the highest place and to receive the lowest ceremonial bows, or of attaching so much importance to titles that they are led into the temptation of authoritarianism and pride. Whatever the ecclesiastical authority he is invested with, a man must take the place, the respect, and the titles which are accorded to him as signs of his office which will contribute to the order and discipline of the Church. But he must guard himself against taking pleasure in them, for that is one of the temptations to which he is exposed in his spiritual life. Christ warns every pastor, confessor, and director against this temptation when he declares: 'But be not ye called Rabbi: for one is your teacher, and all ye are brethren. And call no man your father on the earth: for one is your Father, which is in heaven. Neither be ye called masters: for one is your master, even the Christ. But he that is greatest among you shall be your servant. And whosoever shall exalt himself shall be humbled; and whosoever shall humble himself shall be exalted' (Matt. 23.8-12, RV). The point of this exhortation is not the suppression of all order and hierarchy in the Church—the exhortation itself speaks of the 'greatest among you' and of the exalting of him that humbles himself. Our Lord is pointing out that those who have authority in the Church must consider it in the light of a service to others. The Christian, moreover, must not seek to be exalted, but on the contrary, to humble himself.

Nor do these words of Jesus condemn the order of hierarchical precedence in the Church. A bishop or a superior is invested with an authority which ought to be signified by the place he occupies among the assembled Christian community. A bishop or a superior is obeying his vocation in accepting in all simplicity the first place, and truly serving his brethren in being for them the sign of order and discipline.

Although this text does not exclude hierarchical order, it does warn any man who holds a position of authority in the Church against the temptation of titles and forms. Has the Church always paid sufficient attention to our Lord's warning when, emphasizing that we are all brothers, he exhorts us not to have ourselves called Rabbi (teacher), Father, or Master? There is only one Teacher, Father, and Master. Perhaps even our use of the term 'spiritual director' errs against this instruction in the Gospel, and ought to be renounced in favour of 'spiritual guide'. Guide smacks less of personal authority than director, for it implies collaboration, a communion between pastor and flock which better reserves to Christ alone his place as the one Master. Like that of Master or director, the appellation Father ought also to be excluded from the Christian vocabulary, as applying to the ministers of the Church. Nevertheless the purpose of Christ's words was only to warn and preserve the Church's ministers against the pride to which they might be tempted by certain titles and marks of respect. Though there is inherent in the ministry of confession the danger of developing a certain authoritarianism or a spirit of paternal possessiveness, it must be recognized that it implies on the part of the confessor a legitimate sentiment of spiritual paternity. In denying to the pastor the title of Father, Christ's purpose is to save him from the temptation of possessiveness, and not to forbid him to entertain paternal compassion towards his flock. Indeed, St Paul writes to the Corinthians: 'For though ye should have ten thousand tutors in Christ, yet have ye not many fathers: for in Christ Jesus I begat you through the Gospel' (I Cor. 4.15, RV). The Apostle is here reminding the Corinthian Christians that though they may receive instruction from other masters than he, yet he is the first, and therefore the only one who can claim that spiritual fatherhood which consists in having begotten them in the faith. A sentiment of fatherhood is therefore legitimate in the ministry, but it does not imply possession, which would be jealous of any other teaching that the believer might receive from some other master in Christ. It is a special bond created by God between the pastor and the believer whom he has brought to faith and maintained in obedience. A few lines further on St Paul calls Timothy his 'beloved son, and faithful in the Lord' (I Cor. 4.17; see also Phil. 2.22). And to the Thessalonians St Paul writes: 'Ye know how we exhorted and comforted and charged every one of you, as a father doth his children, that ye would walk worthy of God, who hath called you unto his kingdom and glory' (I Thess. 2.11-12). The spiritual fatherhood of the confessor, therefore, consists not in an authority which might be in danger of becoming possessive, because of the dangerous use of a title, but rather in his duty to exhort with gravity, to console with gentleness, and seriously to adjure believers, in order to bring them to God's kingdom and glory. The spiritual guide watches over the salvation of the souls for whom he will have to render an account, like a father watching over a child.

This extreme vigilance and sensitiveness with regard to a Christian's personal life is one of the qualities most necessary in a confessor.

This sensitivity comes from the experience of his own sin, his own weakness, his own sufferings, and from the ever-faithful grace of God, as well as from the conviction that he is responsible before Christ for those who are entrusted to his ministry. He must beware of fearing and deploring it. On the contrary he must develop and nourish it by frequent meditation upon the love of the crucified Christ. He must daily allow himself to be beset by his care for his ministry, and hold up in intercession those who have chosen him as confessor or spiritual guide. 'Who is weak, and I am not weak? who is offended, and I burn not?' (II Cor. 11.29). Upon the weakness of the believer the confessor should have such compassion that it makes him weak himself; he must share the troubles and sufferings and so understand the situation of the sinner that he can carry his burden with him to cast it on Christ. Knowing the wiles of the Devil, and tempted like any other man, but above all having because of his ministry a sense of his spiritual fatherhood, which makes him look upon the believer as a child to be comforted as well as exhorted and adjured, he suffers the same distress and feels in himself the same weaknesses, which lead him to repentance in common with the believer. If the latter backslides, or is in danger of giving way to a temptation that is too strong for him, the confessor suffers an anxiety which cannot but force him to his knees in intercession. St Paul goes so far as to compare it to a burning fever. The ministry of confession involves this self-giving and this torture of the whole of one's being. These are the manifestations of the compassion that is necessary to real consolation. 'My little children,' writes St Paul to the Galatians, 'of whom I travail in birth again until Christ be formed in you, I desire to be present with you now' (Gal. 4.19-20). Only through prayer and his own confession can the confessor keep himself upright in this battle waged in another for the victory of Christ over the Devil. In the love of Jesus Christ the confessor finds the compassion which burns him and the peace which allows him to convey comfort, to remain patient, and to hope always.

Knowing that he himself is weak and subject to temptation, the confessor can for others be sick with their weakness, and walk on hot embers with him who walks on the edge of the abyss of hell. The confessor can apply to himself the parable of the unjust steward (Luke 16.1-9). He can see himself as the rich man's steward accused by his master of having wasted his goods. In fact, both as Christian and as pastor, he has failed and always fails in love towards God and his neighbour; he does not know how to use for himself or for others the treasures of grace. When he appears before the Master, he feels himself unable to give an account of his stewardship, and deserving of having it taken away from him. Nevertheless, he has one chance left of saving himself: to put himself at the service of his Master's debtors, to lessen their debts. So he will make himself friends, and the Master will commend the unjust steward because he has done wisely. The confessor must make himself the generous dispenser of the Lord's mercy, remitting through absolution the sinner's debts. He is thus the good dispenser of the treasures of God, and does wisely. So his duty is to distribute freely the Lord's grace, and in so doing he encourages the growth of the communion of saints. This indulgence in accordance with the wisdom of the Lord, this generous distribution of forgiveness, does in fact create among the faithful the communion of pardoned sinners. 'Make to yourselves friends by means of the mammon of unrighteousness; that, when it shall fail, they may receive you into eternal tabernacles' (Luke 16.9, RV). Through his ministry the confessor develops the communion of saints by strengthening the bonds which unite the faithful to Christ and to the Church; he gives them new friends by delivering sinners from the burden of their unrighteousness. In absolution he remits the debts of sin and creates the magnificent obligation of grateful thanksgiving. By thus faithfully performing his ministry he saves himself with the faithful, in the communion of saints; and if one day, having preached to others, he himself should be in danger of being a castaway, his ministry and his intercession for sinners would plead for him, and they would receive him into paradise. Confession, absolution, and intercession for sinners are powerful means of building up the communion of saints.

It is a wonderful thing in the solitude of our sinfulness to have at Christ's side a confidant who is not chosen only in view of some human affinity or sympathy, but represents God and the Church with the authority of the ministry to console, exhort, and pardon.[1] How many there are who struggle with insoluble problems, how many overwhelmed by spiritual distress, gnawed by anguish the sharper for being secret, who would find in confession the road to sure liberation which they have despaired of finding. It is good to have among men, in the Church, a brother who knows you as well as he knows himself before God. There are many struggles,

---

[1] 'When the whole congregation stands, as it were, before the judgement seat of God, when they confess themselves guilty, and acknowledge that they have no refuge but in the mercy of God, it is no trivial consolation to have Christ's ambassador present, furnished with the mandate of absolution, by whom they may have their absolution pronounced in the name of his Master, and by his authority' (Calvin, *Institutes*, 1560 edition, Bk. III, Ch. IV, Para. 14). This view of the pastor as Christ's ambassador lies at the root of the Calvinist doctrine of the ministry of confession and absolution.

hesitations, and periods of stagnation in the Christian life, which could be avoided by means of confession, making way for more fruitful service in the Church. 'Therefore,' wrote Calvin, 'let every believer remember, if he feels such secret anguish from a sense of his sins, that he cannot find repose without some exterior aid, to use this remedy, as it is offered him by God: which is, that in order to alleviate his distress, he should first disburden himself to his pastor, whose office it is, both publicly and privately, to comfort the people of God with the doctrine of the Gospel.'

It is only fair, along with the blessings of confession, to point out its dangers. I note them here, not in order to give anyone cause to hesitate over adopting a regular and frequent practice of confession, but to show that I am not unaware that they exist. Too often we see the dangers of a particular course of action aimed at the renewing of the Church's life, even before we have taken the first step along the path, with the result that we never take that step, or any other. It might be a salutary proceeding to put Roman Catholics on their guard against the dangers of confession, but similar warnings to Protestants might incur correspondingly grave risks. For the time being at any rate we need not fear that our members are using confession too much! It is, however, possible that in some cases spiritual direction is being used irresponsibly. There are some who are unwilling to grow up in their Christian life, and who live like parasites on the ministry of the cure of souls, constantly consulting their pastors on trivial matters. The pastor must see to it that he is not monopolized in this way: he owes a duty to all. He will sometimes need to refuse to furnish the counsel they desire, trying to set them free by leading them to their spiritual coming-of-age. The believer for his part must be on his guard against taking pleasure in perpetually talking about himself, a habit which is both spiritually and psychologically harmful.

An important obstacle to confession is the fear that its secrecy may be betrayed. It is the duty of the confessor to keep with the utmost scrupulousness the promise which the Church requires of him at his consecration, to keep secret the confessions which may be made to him for the quieting of conscience. This is not only a matter of refraining from repeating a private confession, which goes without saying. His whole attitude, his words and gestures, as well as any measures he may be called upon to take elsewhere with regard to a person who has made his confession to him, must be such that they will in no way betray the confession that has been made. The Roman Church takes elaborate precautions against the possibility of involuntary or unconscious violation of the seal of confession. She gives her priests advice which we too could profitably take to heart. The secrecy of confession is essential if its practice is to be encouraged. The believer must be imbued with complete confidence, so that he may feel free to confess his most intimate problems. The sacramental seal, the need for absolute and inviolable secrecy imposed on every confessor with regard to everything he hears in confession, has been unequivocally stressed ever since the practice of private confession first began. St Augustine and St Leo were the first to insist categorically upon the necessity of the *sigillum confessionis*.[1] The body of ecclesiastical law concerning the secrecy of the confessional may seem to be casuistry, in the bad sense of that term; in reality it bears witness to the respect the Church has for men's consciences. A bishop or a religious superior cannot use what they have learnt from hearing a confession in order to remove a man from some position of ecclesiastical responsibility for which his confession has shown him to be unfitted.

[1] Concerning the seal of confession, St Augustine says: 'I set before the guilty person the judgement of God, I fright his conscience, I persuade him to (public) penance. We are blamed for sparing a sinner guilty of adultery; it is imagined that we do not know what we do know; but perhaps I do know what you know, and if I do not reprehend that person in public it is because I wish to heal him rather than to accuse him' (*Serm.* LXXXII, Ch. VII, n. 11, P.L., Vol. XXXVIII, Col. 511). Thus St Augustine envisages the usefulness of public confession in certain cases, but he does not make it compulsory; he urges it, but does not break the bond of secrecy.

We have already mentioned St Leo's exhortation concerning the secrecy of confession to the bishops of Campania (see p. 61).

The various ways foreseen by the Roman Church in which the secrecy of confession may be violated are worth studying. They help to show the absolute nature of this rule of secrecy. 'The confessor cannot use the knowledge acquired at the holy tribunal to do anything that might prejudice the penitent or shake the confidence of the faithful in the irrefragable silence of the confessor. Likewise a priest who knows the unworthiness of a person only through confession ought not to refuse him communion either in public or in secret. He may not refuse to proceed to the marriage of persons between whom there exists a diriment impediment, if this is known only through sacramental confession. The bishop may not refuse orders to a person whom he knows to be of irregular life, if this knowledge has been obtained only through confession. The case would be otherwise if these facts were known both sacramentally and by public notoriety. This latter source of information would restore his liberty of action to the confessor. Furthermore, a priest who has refused absolution to an ill-disposed penitent, if he is himself accused of the crime committed by his penitent, may not defend himself by betraying the secrecy of confession, even to the peril of his life.'[1] Obviously the confessor owes it to himself to exhort the penitent to the reparation of his faults, or to resignation from an office of which the sin confessed renders him unworthy or incapable. But whether his exhortation is heeded or not, he can in no wise betray the secret or act in such a way that the secret might be revealed or even its nature suggested. In fact, the confessor has no knowledge of the sin confessed except as God's representative in the special ministry of confession. He has no knowledge of it as a man, as a Christian, or even as an ecclesiastical authority—even if he be a bishop. It is his duty to ignore, outside confession, everything that a penitent may have revealed to him. His silence must be so absolute that he may morally deny a fact known from confession when questioned on the point by someone who wishes to make him reveal the secret, in the very exceptional case of his

[1] B. Dolhagaray, *Dict. Théol. cath.*, Vol. III, 1, Col. 966.

being unable to avoid the question without thereby giving some indication of the truth. It is generally possible to silence such indiscreet questioners by reminding them of the secrecy of confession.

There are some pastors who think they ought to share with their wives some of their parochial responsibilities, and this can indeed bring great enrichment to the labours of the minister of the Church. But it goes without saying, after what has just been said about the seal of confession, that the pastor must maintain a silence just as absolute—being if anything even more careful—in front of his wife. No doctrine of the unity of the partners in marriage can authorize in the very least degree any violation of the secrecy of confession. If the pastor wishes to encourage among his flock the practice of confident confession of sins, he must take care over the circumstances in which confession is to be made. I shall return later to this question, but it must be pointed out here how important the choice of a place for confessions is, in view of the need to ensure secrecy, especially with regard to the pastor's family. It is quite certain that a person will find it easier to come to confession in church, in the vestry, or in some independent office, than in a room in the pastor's house which he cannot enter without the fact being seen and known by the members of the family.

Apart from the fear of secrecy not being observed, people may also be reluctant to come to confession because they fear that the confessor will always remember the sin that has been confessed, and that ordinary everyday relationships with him will become a source of embarrassment. This is a real difficulty, but it can be avoided, however, if the confession is made in an atmosphere of simple brotherly sincerity. The pastor should take this particular fear as a reason for maintaining such control over himself that he will never, even by the most secret look or gesture, remind the penitent that he is aware of what has been confessed. In his prayers he must ask God to grant that these things be blotted out from his memory. The confessor must pray God that the absolution which he addresses to the penitent may act not only upon the spiritual state of the latter, but also be equally as effective on his own mind. When the confession is a real living dialogue between the penitent and God, in the presence of a minister of the Church who realizes that he is not meant to take the burden of sins upon himself, but simply with the penitent to bring them to Christ, who will take their weight upon himself through absolution, then he will more easily be able, through God's grace, to blot them out from his memory. Some confessors do in fact find that they think of the sin of a penitent only at the moment of confession, in intercession, and when they are reflecting upon what spiritual advice they ought to give. Outside the performance of these acts of their proper ministerial function it is given to them to remain simple and natural.

CHAPTER SEVEN

THE PRACTICE OF CONFESSION

EVEN when one is convinced of the rightness of confession, one may come up against various practical difficulties. There is first the danger that habit will gradually weaken, in the long run, the feeling of penitence and the joy of absolution. Let it be said in this connection, as with the Lord's Supper, that one must not look primarily for a psychological emotion. If absolution has sacramental value, it produces its supernatural effect of the remission of sins and of reconciliation with God, renewing our fellowship with Christ and our communion with the whole Church, independently of any mental feeling. The joy and peace that we feel are, like contrition, further gifts which God may grant to us, but they are not essential to the reality of the confession. Conviction of sin, sincere repentance, and faith in the mercy of God suffice to make our confession a true one. The Lord's Supper and confession are not rendered more valid because of our being emotionally stirred by them. Christ is present and our sins are remitted without our sensibilities first needing to be excited.

To escape the effects of habit, and the consequent risk that we might miss the depth of the sacramental mystery, we must—for confession as well as for Communion—refresh ourselves in prayer, meditation, and self-examination.

A second difficulty is the fact that our sins tend to repeat themselves, so that we find ourselves obliged to confess the same things over and over again. This may be due to a faulty self-examination, to allowing our minds to become as it were fog-bound, unable to see beyond one particular sin that besets us. It is the duty of the spiritual director to draw the attention of the penitent to a sin of which he is unaware, or which he has passed over in silence, because we tend to be blinded by some fault which may be less serious in spite of its preoccupying our minds. However, it remains true that we are not liberated completely overnight from a particular sin by absolution. It must be remembered that the primary purpose of absolution is not psychological liberation, but the spiritual assurance of God's forgiveness. Even if we know that deliverance will not be rapid, we must ask for forgiveness and in faith receive the remission of sins. Absolution may be compared to a medicine which we must take in order to go on living, even while realizing that it is not going to heal us at once. The assurance of Christ's mercy, which is nurtured in us by absolution, is essential to a full Christian life. The Christian therefore will seek it in order to deepen his spiritual life, even if he does not find himself freed from a sin which he is obliged to go on confessing repeatedly. It is necessary also to see sacramental absolution as a mystery which, by bringing us back to life in Christ, brings us into contact with the world to come. As in the Lord's Supper, we find ourselves in an eschatological situation. In anticipation we witness Christ's return, and at the moment of the sacrament are clothed with the holiness and purity which will be granted to us in full measure by the Lord in the last day. In one and the same epistle St John is able to say: 'If we say that we have no sin, we deceive ourselves and the truth is not in us. If we confess our sins, he is faithful and just to forgive us our sins and to cleanse us from all unrighteousness. If we say that we have not sinned, we make him a liar, and his word is not in us. . . . And ye know that he was manifested to take away our sins; and in him is no sin. Whosoever abideth in him sinneth not: whosoever sinneth hath not seen him, neither known him' (I John 1.8-10; 3.5-6). How are we to understand this paradox in the unity of the faith? The mystery of absolution makes it possible to understand it. Truth compels us to recognize that our human nature wallows in sin, and moves us to confess it in order to be forgiven and purified. We still remain sinners—often the same sinner has to confess the same sin again and again. Through sacramental absolution we are transported into Christ, in whom there is no sin; and if we abide in him, that is to say as long as in anticipation we live the return of Christ, we have no sin; if we begin to sin once more, it is because our contemplation is interrupted and our knowledge of him becomes blurred. We are then as if we had not truly seen or known him. The sacramental mystery of confession is like a necessary bath which washes us, but does not stop us getting dirty again. Only the extension into our lives of the faith and obedience of the sacrament can make it possible for us to win partial victory in this world and final victory at the Second Coming of our Lord Jesus Christ. This tension between sacrament, which brings us into contact with the other world, and life, which immerses us in the world of time, makes us express, like the early Christians, our great hope: 'Maranatha, come Lord, the Lord comes.'

Humiliating though the repetition of our sins in confession may be, we must see it as a normal condition of our fallen human nature, and as a sign of the sincerity of our desire for salvation. Confession thus becomes a training in vigilance over sin and temptation, and in fervour, true joy and peace in the assurance of the mercy and love of Christ. Just as we communicate frequently or regularly, so we will submit to a discipline of confession which will vary in accordance with our own temperament and spiritual needs.

Again, confession may be considered as a sort of exorcism in which Christ does battle against the powers of evil. Absolution scatters the devils, re-establishing in the heart the single kingship of Jesus Christ. Since, as the Gospel says, the Christian knows that the devils sometimes return in greater numbers to the place from which they have been driven, he must be ever more vigilant and diligent in the practice of confession as he grows in the spiritual life. The Church has lost the practice of exorcism, and with it the sense of the dramatic struggle that is taking place in the world between herself and Satan. She often thinks that she has to struggle politically against men or against governments in order to manifest the lordship of Jesus Christ. But 'our wrestling is not against flesh and blood, but against the principalities, against the powers, against the world-rulers of this darkness, against the spiritual hosts of wickedness in the heavenly places' (Eph. 6.12, RV). If the Church recovers this sense of being engaged in a supernatural struggle, she will be able to face events and systems in the world with a greater freedom and tranquillity, to work for the conversion of men with a surer hope, knowing that behind events, systems, and men there are principalities, powers, rulers and spirits of darkness using them as pawns in their struggle, but against which she wields the most potent weapon: the Cross of Christ before which Satan takes to flight. So she is more certain of victory than if she used human, temporal, and political means, because she knows before she enters the fray that the victory is already won. The exorcism of confession can restore to the Church a real sense of this supernatural struggle.[1]

The actual practice of confession raises several important problems. It is impossible to be too careful over the preliminaries. Where can the confession take place? How is it to be heard? How is absolution to be given?

As to the place of confession, one must be completely free to choose the place that is best suited to the character and temperament of the penitent. Some will prefer to make their confession in the form of a personal conversation with their pastor. He will find it best to receive them in his office or study, provided it is sufficiently separate from the rest of the house, and he can have visitors there without their being too easily observed by the members of his household. If this cannot be arranged, the pastor may make known the times when he may be seen in the vestry of the church. It is important that those who have not made a regular habit of confession, and have no chance of arranging an interview with the pastor, should know the day and time when he is available for confessions. In this way the often delicate matter of

---

[1] On the cure of souls as exorcism see E. Thurneysen, *op. cit.*, pp. 294-312. 'The receiving of forgiveness,' he writes, 'must finally be understood as an exorcism. The devils are driven away when the Word of God is proclaimed with power' (p. 296).

broaching the subject will be greatly eased. Even when the confession is made in the form of a conversation in this way, the confessor must listen much and speak but little, so as to avoid the mixing of spiritual direction with the confession. He should be content merely to put a question now and then in order to facilitate the process of self-examination. The absolution must always be liturgical in form, to underline its sacramental objectivity.

Though it ought to be possible to practise confession in varying conditions, quite simply and naturally, it will tend gradually to become liturgical in form, and this for many will be a practical help in making it easier, as well as making clearer the necessary distinction between direction and confession. Without going so far as to use a confessional, care should be taken to make it easier for human modesty to reach the point of opening the heart completely. Everything should be done as simply as possible, but without detracting from the objective and ecclesiastical nature of confession. Indeed, it is at once easier and more right to confess to God in the presence of a minister of the Church, than to recount the details of one's life to a man who remains something of a stranger.

The most usual practice is for the confession to be made kneeling beside the confessor, who is also kneeling. In this way we show that it is God, to whom both are looking, who is to hear the confession of the sin; the confessor is but the Church's witness, charged with the ministry of reconciliation. In the church one will kneel in the chancel; elsewhere, in front of a cross or some other symbol of the presence or acts of God.

The penitent asks a blessing:

'Brother, give me thy blessing.'

The confessor pronounces the blessing:

'The Lord be in thy heart and on thy lips that thou mayest truly confess all thy sins, in the Name of the Father, and of the Son, and of the Holy Ghost. Amen.'

Then the penitent begins the liturgical confession:

'I confess to Almighty God, in the communion of the saints in heaven and on earth, and before thee, brother, that I have sinned exceedingly in thought, word, and deed. . . .'

Here the penitent, having prepared himself by self-examination, will admit his sins. The confessor may put a few questions, if necessary, in order to make the confession more sincere. The penitent will conclude as follows:

'. . . It is my fault, my own fault, my own most grievous fault; wherefore I beg thee, brother, in the communion of the saints in heaven and on earth, to pray for me to the Lord our God.'

The confessor, after such exhortation as is necessary, then says the prayer for absolution:

'Almighty God have mercy upon thee, and having forgiven thee thy sins bring thee to everlasting life.'

Then he rises and stands in front of the kneeling penitent, to recall the institution of the ministry of reconciliation, and to give absolution in God's name:

'The Lord breathed on his disciples and said unto them, Receive ye the Holy Ghost:

'Whose soever sins ye remit, they are remitted unto them; and whose soever sins ye retain, they are retained.

'May our Lord Jesus Christ absolve thee; and I by his authority do absolve thee from every bond of sin.

'Thus do I grant thee absolution from thy sins, in the Name of the Father, and of the Son, and of the Holy Ghost. Amen.'

The formula of absolution is two-fold, for it reconciles the Christian with the Church, and this reconciliation is the sign that God has forgiven, according to the words of Jesus when he said: 'Whose soever sins ye remit, they are remitted unto them' (John 20.23). The formula of absolution stresses the fact that it is the Lord who gives absolution, in answer to our prayer; but absolution is not only a prayer, it is an effective sign. By Christ's authority, the minister has power to absolve the penitent, to reconcile him with the Church, and to assure him of God's forgiveness.

The reference to the bond recalls the impediment formed by

sin in the life of the community, and the state of spiritual 'excommunication' in which it places us. Absolution removes this impediment and breaks the bond of excommunication; it gives back liberty to the captive.

The alternating affirmations of the sole authority and of the power of the Church underline well the mystery of the sacrament, in which God, who is free to bestow his grace as he wills, allows himself to be bound to the acts and words of the Church, of a consecrated man. The 'I' does not refer to any personal power possessed by the confessor. It draws attention to the fact that absolution is not merely an announcement, a word preached, but a fact, an act, a sacrament. With that 'I' the ministry of the Church joins her Lord in the declaration of the forgiveness which brings peace.[1]

As the confessor recites the first part of the absolution he may lay his hands on the penitent, as a concrete sign of the act which is being performed, although the sacrament of absolution does not consist in the laying on of hands, which is optional, but in the word which looses. Then, in those traditions where it is practised (Roman, Orthodox, Anglican, and Lutheran), the confessor may make the sign of the cross upon the penitent as he recites the Name of the Trinity. This sign recalls Baptism in the Name of the Father, the Son, and the Holy Ghost, of which absolution is the re-presentation. It recalls also the Cross through which the Lord showed his mercy upon us once for all. 'Father, forgive them; for they know not what they do' (Luke 23.34). Lastly it reminds us that confession and absolution constitute a sort of exorcism, by

[1] Calvin looks upon the person of the pastor as a surety, 'to certify our consciences of the remission of sins'. Luther, too, uses a formula in which the 'I', far from signifying that the pastor has personal power to forgive, is a sure and effective sign of the certainty of God's mercy: 'The confessor shall say: May God be merciful to thee and strengthen thy faith! Amen. Believest thou that my forgiveness is the forgiveness of God?— The penitent shall reply: Yes, dear Master.—And then the confessor shall say: According to thy faith be it done unto thee. And I, by the commandment of our Lord Jesus Christ, do forgive thee thy sins, in the Name of the Father, the Son, and the Holy Ghost. Amen. Go in peace' (*Little Catechism*; see my Conclusion).

which the devils are driven out in the Name of the crucified and risen Christ.

The confessor then proceeds with a prayer in the same spirit: 'The Passion of our Lord Jesus Christ be for thee the only source of remission of sins, the increase of faith, and the reward of eternal life. Amen.' Then he may add an act of thanksgiving and a prayer for the perseverance of the penitent. He concludes with the words:

'Thy sins are forgiven; thy faith hath saved thee; go in peace!'

If the confession is made in church, the confessor will withdraw, leaving the penitent to pray. It is preferable for the confessor and the penitent to separate at once. If spiritual direction is necessary, it can be given on a subsequent occasion. If for practical reasons the spiritual direction must follow immediately upon confession, reference must not be made to the confession as if the sin were unforgiven. It may be necessary to take up again some matter mentioned in the confession: such references must be made with delicacy, the penitent being given to understand that a sin, though forgiven, may leave behind psychological traces, and that steps must be taken to avoid fresh temptation. Further, it may be necessary to advise the penitent to admit a fault to some other person and ask his forgiveness, or to repair some damage caused by the sin. All this follows absolution, and the impression must not be given that forgiveness is conditional upon it: forgiveness is freely given. The spiritual direction which follows confession must rather trace out the path of gratitude, obedience, and thanksgiving.

The confession must not be confined to a general admission of sin. It must be precise and concrete. Its value does not, of course, depend on an exhaustive enumeration of the wrongdoings committed, but it is important to make the state of sin clear, precise, and concrete, through the confession of particular and significant faults. It is easy and superficial to say that one is proud, selfish, and impure. Such confessions must be made real by reference to specific occasions on which these sins showed themselves. It often happens that the power of Satan and of temptation is weakened by a more circumstantial and detailed confession, through the disgust with himself that it arouses in the penitent. There are things which, when put into words, lose their evil attraction, so that the more one speaks of them the less desire one has to do them. Mystery and secrecy exert a great power of attraction over us. This is as true in confession as elsewhere. As long as men still cast a veil of mystery over some sinful propensity in their natures, they enhance its power to tempt them and increase the attraction the sin has for them. If they are willing to make a detailed admission of every fault, the atmosphere of mystery is removed, and so the power of the temptation and the attraction of the sin are broken. It is well known how in impossible or illicit love affairs mystery can exacerbate the temptation, and how one seeks to preserve this atmosphere of mystery so long as one has not crucified the flesh with its affections and lusts. Only frequent and detailed confession is able gradually to remove the mystery and diminish the taste for secrecy—that is to say that such confession alone can deliver us from the temptation of the sin and the anguish of the unsatisfied desire.

The confessor will find it necessary to make the confession more precise and concrete by discreet questioning; he must be prudent on his own account not to give way to curiosity and allow himself to be attracted in his turn by the atmosphere of mystery. This is a real danger, which might eventually arouse disgust in him and lead him to abandon a ministry of confession which has become for him a burden and an occasion for sin.

Prayer, fasting, a redoubling of unselfish love for men, and a longing to bring them to Christ can alone preserve the confessor from this temptation. But he must ever be on his guard and desire only the peace and joy of others.

Is it possible, in self-examination and confession, to make a distinction between different kinds of sin, the grave and the not so grave, venial and mortal sins?

As we have seen, it is important to make a distinction between weakness and sin, so as to avoid the situation in which a guilt-complex makes us confess weaknesses of which we are all the more the victims because we look upon them as sins. The boundary between them is, of course, hard to draw, since a psychological or physical weakness is an occasion of sin which one is not always capable of controlling. Nevertheless it is important that theoretically the distinction should be made, in order to avoid the guilt-complex which is harmful to true confession, since it is a way of escaping a proper examination of real sin.

How many young men there are, who, having been brought up in a certain school of Christian moralism, see sin only as masturbation, and as a result succumb to it all the more often. Their real sin is perhaps a lack of generous love towards God in a regular discipline of prayer, and towards their fellows in true and unselfish sacrifice.

Reformed moral theology does not admit the distinction between venial and mortal sins. Is it right? Protestantism argues that the distinction as made by Roman Catholicism tends to minimize the importance of venial sin. It considers that Roman Catholics are inclined to take such sins too lightly, since it is not 'absolutely necessary' to confess them to a priest. This is a real danger, and we must not minimize it either from a desire to avoid controversy or on the ground of our admiration for certain saintly Roman Catholics.

While this danger of a lack of moral seriousness is a feature of ordinary Catholic thinking, must we not also recognize that there is in the Protestant moral outlook a certain lack of concern with regard to sin? As a result of the belief that there are no venial sins, and that all sins are equally grave in the sight of the holy God, all sin being mortal because it separates us from Christ, one becomes dangerously inured, in the absence of a habit of confession, to the idea of being in a constant state of mortal sin. *Sempter justus, semper peccator* is an assertion which, though true, it is easy to misuse. There grows up a habit of sin which may lead either to neurotic anxiety in association with a guilt-complex, or else to moral negligence, in which one finds it easy to satisfy oneself with a scrap of prayer said in bed at night.

The danger in Roman Catholic moral theology lies in the fact that it defines mortal sin, and consequently venial sin also. 'One commits a mortal sin when one disobeys the law of God in a grave matter, with full knowledge and consent. Such sin is called mortal because it deprives the soul of the life of grace, makes us enemies of God and deserving of the pains of hell. If one has had the misfortune to commit a mortal sin, it is necessary to make an act of contrition, to confess, and to take steps to avoid falling into it again.

'One commits a venial sin when one disobeys the law of God in a trivial matter, or else in a grave matter without entire knowledge or without full consent. Venial sin does not destroy the life of grace, but it inclines us to mortal sin, and makes us deserving of temporal punishment in this world or in the next.'[1]

The difficulty is where to draw the line between grave and trivial matters, between entire and lesser knowledge, between full consent and partial consent. St John teaches that 'whosoever sinneth hath not seen [God], neither known him' (I John 3.6). Thus in his view all sin makes us enemies of God and separates us from Christ. Nevertheless, not all sin is mortal: 'If any man see his brother in a sin not unto death, he shall ask, and [God] shall give him life for them that sin not unto death. There is a sin unto death: I do not say that he shall pray for it. All unrighteousness is sin: and there is a sin not unto death' (I John 5.16-17).

The Apostle wishes us to understand the infinite mercy of God, who does not punish every sinner with eternal death as one might expect, all sin being rebellion against God. We can pray for the forgiveness of sins, for God is merciful and desires not the death of a sinner, but rather that he may turn from his wickedness and

[1] *Catéchisme à l'usage des diocèses de France*, Tardy, Bourges, 1938, pp. 138-9.

live. Nevertheless there is a prayer which St John does not recommend—that for the conversion of the damned, of Satan and the devils. They have committed a sin which has led them to eternal death. God's decision is irrevocable: they will be destroyed in the 'second death' (Rev. 20.14-15).

But St John does not define mortal sin nor refer in specific terms to any particular sin as being mortal. Nor does he even describe the moral conditions from which mortal sin might be recognized. 'There is a sin unto death,' he says, and the mystery remains. The Gospel is no more precise when it speaks of blasphemy against the Holy Ghost, in a passage which should be compared with what St John says about the 'sin unto death.' In St Mark's Gospel Jesus says: 'Verily I say unto you, All their sins shall be forgiven unto the sons of men, and their blasphemies wherewith soever they shall blaspheme: but whosoever shall blaspheme against the Holy Spirit hath never forgiveness, but is guilty of an eternal sin' (Mark 3.28-9, RV; see also Matt. 12.31-2; Heb. 6.4-6; 10.26-9; I Tim. 1.12-13). This blasphemy against the Holy Ghost, a mortal sin, is the rejection of Christ in full knowledge of the situation. It is not the sin of the unbelieving or the indifferent who act 'ignorantly in unbelief' (I Tim. 1.13), and who perhaps speak 'against the Son of man' (Matt. 12.32) because they do not know him intimately, enlightened by the Holy Ghost, but only as a prophet, as a man, not as God and Saviour. The blasphemy against the Holy Ghost is the sin which Christians can commit, who having been 'once enlightened', having 'tasted of the heavenly gift' and been 'made partakers of the Holy Ghost, and . . . tasted the good word of God, and the powers of the world to come . . . crucify to themselves the Son of God afresh, and put him to an open shame' (Heb. 6.4-6). Such apostasy seems impossible and incredible to the Christian. But it is there as a threat. After all, who is there who, in spite of being filled with the Holy Spirit and with grace, has never felt the irresistible attraction of wilful sin? What Christian is there who can say that if all the barriers were down he could still victoriously resist even the most vulgar temptation? Such a fall could mean his apostasy. 'For if we sin wilfully after that we have received knowledge of the truth, there remaineth no more sacrifice for sins' (Heb 10.26). The blasphemy against the Holy Ghost, the sin unto death, is that of him who has 'trodden under foot the Son of God, and hath counted the blood of the covenant, wherewith he was sanctified, an unholy thing, and hath done despite unto the Spirit of grace' (Heb. 10.29).

Here again the Scriptures do not define any specific sin, nor do they indicate the conditions of gravity, knowledge, or consent which make this sin mortal. We know only that it is the sin— possible though hard to believe—of the Christian only, and that it is the rejection of Christ in full knowledge of what we are doing, and that it makes further repentance a practical impossibility. This mortal sin, therefore, is to be recognized from its possible author (the Christian), and by its immediate and secondary consequences (apostasy and hardening of the heart respectively).

Though every sin and every blasphemy may be forgiven, ought we not to agree with Roman Catholic moral teaching in saying that any sin can lead us into (or actually *be*) mortal blasphemy against the Holy Ghost, and then to refuse, on the grounds of this assertion itself, to make any theoretical distinction between mortal and venial sins? All sin is grave, all sin may lead to (or become) the sin which brings us to death; all sin, of whatever kind, must be confessed if it is present in the mind. Thus, by denying the distinction between venial and mortal sins we avoid the danger of taking sin too lightly, and by asserting that on the same grounds all sin must be confessed we also avoid the danger of moral negligence.

There is no venial sin. There are only sins which separate us from Christ, and which must all be confessed in order that we may receive the assurance of reconciliation with God. Any given sin may, for a particular Christian, become mortal, may lead to apostasy and make further repentance impossible. It is not possible to specify under what conditions this mortal sin will be committed; one can only affirm its existence and show its consequences.[1]

In several places St Paul draws up a list of sins, and declares that 'they which do such things shall not inherit the kingdom of God' (I Cor. 6.9-10; Gal. 5.19-21). These are not exhaustive lists of mortal sins, but the Apostle wishes to put in concrete terms the extreme forms which sin may take, and to emphasize that those who take pleasure in such excesses may incur the penalty of eternal death. These lists, along with those of the Christian virtues (Gal. 5.22-3) and the Ten Commandments (Ex. 20.3-17), may serve as a guide for self-examination.

Guidance of this sort in self-examination is useful for the beginner in the regular practice of confession, or for a spiritual retreat. I give an example in the pages which follow. It should not be taken as a questionnaire to which one answers 'Yes' or 'No', but as an aid to clarity and sincerity in one's thoughts about oneself. Sometimes one may read each question, while on another occasion the headings alone will be enough to stimulate the examination. The aim is finally to reach the stage at which self-examination is practised freely, without the necessity of a guide, because one has learnt to be clear-sighted and honest, and has come fully to trust one's confessor as a friend, without forgetting that he is the minister of the Lord and of the Church.

[1] Calvin, refusing to accept the distinction between mortal and venial sin which was made by the moral theology of his day, writes: 'On the contrary, we, as the Scripture (which is the measure of good and evil) teaches us, declare that the wages of sin is death, and that *the soul that has sinned is worthy of death*; moreover, that *the sins of the faithful are venial*: not that they do not merit death, but inasmuch as in the mercy of God *there is no condemnation to them which are in Christ Jesus*: inasmuch as their sins are not imputed to them, but are *blotted out by grace*' (*Institutes*, Bk. III, Ch. IV, Para. 28).

This is basically the same conclusion as that to which we have come here. We can say, with Calvin, that all sins are at once mortal and venial: mortal because they merit death, venial because all can be pardoned.

Calvin cannot conceive of a sin becoming really mortal in a Christian, because according to his doctrine of double predestination, he does not believe it possible to lose faith. But at that point I do not think that he remains faithful to Scripture, in spite of the beauty and grandeur of his system.

SELF-EXAMINATION

Prayer of Preparation for Confession

Psalm

One of the following penitential psalms may be read: 6, 32, 38, 51, 102, 130, 143.

Prayer for Light

O my Lord and my God, source of light, you who know my misery and my sin, grant me your Holy Spirit that he may illuminate my heart and mind, that by his light I may truly see all my sins as clearly as I shall see them when on leaving this life I must stand to be judged before you. Make me see, O holy God, the evil I have done and the good I have left undone; the full extent of my unfaithfulness in your service; how often and to what extent I have wronged my neighbour and myself; and all my omissions of duty.

Enlighten me, and suffer not, O God of truth, the self-love wherewith I am possessed to seduce and blind me. Take away the veil which it puts before my eyes, that nothing may hinder me from knowing myself, from revealing myself as much as is necessary to my brethren, from making known to my confessor all my guilt, and from having before you true sorrow for having offended you, true repentance for my sinful state, and true faith in the complete absolution which you have promised me.

Bring me to the foot of the Saviour's cross, that I may contemplate in Christ Crucified the punishment which by my sins I have deserved:

I who ought to be in his place,
nailed to the wood,
condemned to death,

and that I may contemplate also your love which desires not

the death of a sinner, but rather that he may turn again and live, and which makes you give yourself for me in the suffering of Calvary in Jesus Christ your Son, our Lord. Amen.

Self-examination

The following may be used for meditation: Matt. 5.17-48; Gal. 5.13 to 6.5; I Cor. 13.

I. Love for God

1. Do I love Christ with a love that passes all love?

2. Have I in my heart, in imagination or in truth, another God than he?

3. Is Christ truly living for me, at my side and in my mind?

4. Have I true joy in the love of Christ for me, and do I long to make it known to others?

5. Do I set aside daily a regular period of time for private prayer and converse with Christ?

6. Do I keep truly holy one day in the week, in more fervent prayer to God, and a deeper knowledge of the life of the Holy Spirit within me, in true rest which makes me desire the return of Christ and eternal life with him?

(The first four commandments: Ex. 20.3-11; Matt. 12.29-30).

II. Love for the Church

1. Do I look upon the Church as the Body of Christ, and have I a great love for her, particularly for my own denomination and the parish or community to which I belong, knowing that Christ loved the Church and gave himself for her?

2. Do I love the people and the ministers of my Church, or am I easily irritated by their imperfections?

3. Do I make an effort to appreciate the community life and worship of my parish and the preaching of my pastor, not indulging constantly in carping criticism, but rather making the best contribution I can to the renewal of the Church?

4. Do I give sufficiently of my time and money to help the

growth of the life of the Church, compared with the time and money I spend on my pleasures?

5. Am I too sectarian or partisan in my attachment to a particular Christian tradition, despising those who do not believe or worship exactly as I do? Do I criticize them and want them to be discomfited, instead of having, while still being loyal to my Church, a faith that overcomes prejudices and is open to new possibilities in the Church's life, and hopes fervently for the visible unity of the Churches, working and praying for it?

6. Do I truly respect the pastors and Church authorities? Do I obey and submit to those who have the spiritual rule over me, knowing that they watch on behalf of my soul, as they that shall have to give account, so that they may perform their ministry with joy? (Heb. 13.17).

7. Do I make an effort to know and understand the faith, the catechism and the doctrine of the Church, submitting my personal opinions to them, or do I content myself with vague beliefs or purely individual, sectarian, or heretical theories?

8. Have I any doubts about the fundamental truths of the Christian faith?

III. Love for my Neighbour

1. Do I love my neighbour irrespective of the sort of person he is or his position in life? Do I act as a brother towards him?

2. Am I able to forgive quickly and forget a wrong done to me?

3. Do I try to live in love and charity with my neighbour, and do I seek at once and eagerly to put things right with him, whether it is I who have offended him, or he me?

4. Am I patient, kind, good, faithful, meek? (Gal. 5.22).

5. Do I try to get more than I give in loving my neighbour, to be loved rather than to love freely, expecting nothing in return?

6. Do I easily become bitter when I see the ingratitude and selfishness of some other person, instead of having the peace of being thus united with Christ in his abandonment on the Cross?

7. Am I too ready to think evil of my neighbour or my brother,

instead of excusing all things, believing all things, hoping all things, enduring all things? (I Cor. 13.5-7).

8. Have I a spirit of sacrifice towards my neighbour? Am I the one who serves, or the one who likes to be served (exacting and lazy)?

9. Am I sufficiently brotherly, open-hearted, ready to help anyone, to give myself generously, to give all my time to the lowliest person who needs my help?

10. When I seek Christ in my brothers, do I do so in true brotherly love, forgetting my own advantage? Or is it only an excuse to satisfy my desire to love selfishly and to be loved exclusively?

11. Have I a true spirit of obedience towards those set over me? Do I try to work with them rather than criticizing them and paying no attention to them?

12. Do I act lovingly, justly, and reasonably towards my children, or towards those placed under my authority, knowing that by their subordinate position they are showing me that humility which is a condition of entry into the Kingdom of Heaven?

13. Have I a real concern for social justice? Am I doing my utmost to put an end to inequalities which are an offence in Christ's eyes?

14. Am I careful to avoid giving offence to my neighbour by my failure in true Christian living or in human sympathy, or by cowardly silence, or loose speech, voluntarily or involuntarily, or by my spirit of contradiction?

15. Do I truly love and respect my parents?

IV. Personal Life

A. *Humility*

1. Do I look upon myself as the centre of any company in which I happen to be?

2. Do I seek admiration and praise without being able easily to bear remarks and criticisms?

3. Am I boastful in conversations?

4. Am I able really to look upon others as superior to myself?

5. Do I love to take first place?

6. Have I a thoughtless—possibly unconscious—love of authority, power, or domination?

7. Can I allow others to have different opinions from my own, without flying into a temper or despising them?

8. Do I really try to understand other people and to see their point of view?

9. Am I able to forget myself so that others may be seen in a more favourable light? Or do I take pleasure in the intellectual, physical, or social inferiority, and the misfortunes of others? Am I complacent about injustice done to others? Do I relish conversations which show my own superiority and give me a chance to show off and reveal myself in a favourable light?

10. Do I feed my egoism by being hail-fellow-well-met with everybody?

B. *Generosity*

1. Am I selfishly unresponsive, enigmatic, taciturn towards others?

2. Do I find it hard to give of myself, my time, my labour, my goods?

3. Am I over-scrupulous and fussy in everything relating to my belongings, or am I on the contrary untidy and unmethodical under the pretext of being generous? Am I a bad steward of the goods that God has entrusted to me?

4. Am I too easy-going with regard to other people's belongings, not realizing that what I am doing may really amount to stealing?

5. Do I misuse what has been entrusted to me or what belongs to me by squandering it?

6. Have I a real respect for the economic discipline of this world (taxes, customs dues, etc.), and am I not too ready to allow myself a licence in this respect which amounts to dishonesty?

7. Do I remain faithful to the spirit of poverty and simplicity

enjoined by the Gospel, or is my life hampered by my goods, by material preoccupations, or by a superfluity of worldly belongings?

C. *Purity*

1. Is my love for Christ strong enough to stop me from adding to his suffering by premeditated and frequent infidelity?

2. Do I fully realize that my body is the temple of the Holy Spirit, and that I no longer belong to myself?

3. Do I banish impure thoughts and imaginings, or do I take pleasure in them?

4. Do I lend myself to lewd conversations, readings, attitudes, and spectacles, and anything which panders to my sensual emotions?

5. Do I respect women in thought, word, and deed, knowing that whosoever looks on a woman to lust after her has committed adultery already with her in his heart?

6. Are my friendships honest, whole-hearted, unselfish, and unsentimental?

7. Do I allow myself to be a cause of temptation because of my failure to maintain a high standard of behaviour?

8. As a bachelor or celibate, do I uphold the ideal of purity in fellowship with Christ, conscious of the power of chastity to shed abroad the love of Christ?

9. As a married man, do I hold the sexual life in honour, and am I able freely and with simplicity to face all its problems together with my wife, in obedience to Christ?

10. Am I convinced that liberation is almost always the fruit of confession? Do I desire to have a confessor from whom I want to hide absolutely nothing, subjecting myself to a strict discipline of confession?

11. Am I willing to bring my body into subjection in order to keep it pure: energy without over-work, prudence without prudery, prompt and early rising, prayer before retiring, hygiene, orderliness, manners, physical exercise, fasting, frequent communion? (I Cor. 9.24-7).

12. Am I ready to break off certain relations, friendships, and correspondence, where this is necessary?

D. *Unselfishness*

1. Have I an inordinate desire for that which it has not yet been given me to possess, or which I shall never have?

2. Am I ready and willing to give up everything to God if he should call me to do so?

3. Am I easily roused to jealousy of the intelligence, position, success, friendship, and love of others?

4. Do I waste energy which ought to be used in Christ's service, in desire, envy, jealousy, and suspicion?

E. *Sobriety*

1. Do I use God's gifts as they ought to be used, freely and with thankfulness, or am I too fond of good food, drink, and tobacco?

2. Am I 'crazy' about some sport or pleasure, so that I find it difficult to do without it?

3. Am I restrained in my speech? Am I able to abstain from smutty jokes or from constantly playing the fool?

F. *Self-control*

1. Can I check my reactions by imposing silence upon myself, both inwardly and outwardly?

2. Do I at once wish to be forgiven by a brother to whom I have spoken harshly, or in anger?

3. When I want to be forgiven, or to 'make it up' with a brother, is this because I am afraid that if the quarrel is allowed to continue it may be made public, to my shame, rather than because I honestly long for the true peace which only forgiveness by God and my neighbour can bring?

4. Do I derive pleasure from arguments, divisions, and parties, which give me a chance to show my aggressiveness and to satisfy my pride and selfishness?

5. Do I believe, as Christ said, that anger is like murder?

G. *Zeal*

1. Am I convinced that true work consists of humble and un-remitting effort?

2. Am I too ready to think myself tired?

3. Am I disciplined about sleep, going to bed and getting up?

4. When I am tired and discouraged can I still muster the strength to be charitable?

5. Am I always 'moaning' about my life and my work, instead of considering them as things of beauty to be carried through manfully without snivelling?

H. *Truth*

1. Have I failed in frankness or truth in speaking to my superiors, my friends, my wife, in order to avoid a punishment, a reproof, or the necessity of giving something up?

2. Do I tell lies in order to show off, or through vanity?

3. Am I often hypocritical, hiding my true thoughts or feelings from my neighbour in order to gain some advantage?

4. Do I love the truth, or do I allow myself to live 'in the dark' through laziness, negligence, or indifference?

Conclusion

1. Have I truly and sincerely sought to know my character and to recognize my besetting sin, in order to admit it frankly and completely?

2. Do I live in a dream-world, dreaming of extraordinary and heroic sacrifices, but being slack about my own work?

3. Have I a true and burning desire to conquer my sins?

4. Have I faith in God's mercy and my need for absolution?

After the self-examination, before confession:

Prayers

O God, whose property is always to have mercy and to forgive, receive my prayer, that your merciful goodness may with clemency absolve me, your unhappy servant, from the fetters of my sin.

Lord, I ask you to grant the prayers of your humble servant, and to remit the sins of him who puts his trust in you, that I may receive, of your goodness, pardon and peace.

Lord, in your clemency, show me your unspeakable mercy, that I may be both delivered from all my sins and spared from the consequences I justly deserve because of them.

O God, who are angered by sin, and who rejoices over the sinner that repents, favourably hear the prayers of your suppliant servant, and turn from me the judgement, which I rightly deserve for my sins.

O God, from whom all holy desires, all good counsels, and all just works do proceed: give unto your servant that peace which the world cannot give; that both my heart may be set to obey your commandments, and also that by you being defended from the fear of my enemies I may pass my time in rest and quietness.

Lord, burn my senses and my heart with the fire of your Holy Spirit, so that I may serve you with a pure body, and please you with a true heart.

O God, the Creator and Redeemer of all faithful people, grant to the soul of your servant the remission of all his sins, so that by his ardent supplications he may obtain the mercy which he ever desires, through Jesus Christ, our Lord, who lives and reigns with you, in the unity of the Holy Spirit, ever one God world without end. Amen.

Confession

Blessing

R̕. Brother, give me the blessing of the Lord.

V̕. The Lord be in your heart and on your lips, that you may truly confess all your sins, in the Name of the Father, and of the Son, and of the Holy Spirit.

Amen.

Confession

.I confess to Almighty God, in the communion of the saints in heaven and on earth, and before you, brother, that I have sinned exceedingly in thought, word, and deed ... (Here the penitent makes his confession, and then concludes:) It is my fault, my own fault, my own most grievous fault; wherefore I beg you, brother, in the communion of the saints in heaven and on earth, to pray for me to the Lord our God.

(The confessor may ask such questions and make such exhortation as is necessary.)

Absolution

℣. Almighty God have mercy upon you, and having forgiven you your sins bring you to everlasting life.

℟. Amen.

(The confessor rises and stands in front of the penitent.)

℣. The Lord breathed on his disciples and said unto them, Receive the Holy Spirit: Whose soever sins you remit, they are remitted unto them; and whose soever sins you retain, they are retained.

(The confessor may lay his hands on the penitent.)

May our Lord Jesus Christ absolve you; and I by his authority do absolve you from every bond of sin.

Thus do I grant you absolution from your sins, in the Name of the Father, and of the Son, and of the Holy Spirit. Amen.

Prayer

The Passion of our Lord Jesus Christ be for you the only source of remission of sins, the increase of faith, and the reward of eternal life. Amen.

Dismissal

Your sins are forgiven; your faith has saved you; go in peace!

After Confession

1. Practical resolutions to be carried out as soon as possible: Ask forgiveness of one's neighbour.

Admit to one's neighbour a wrong done to him.

Act of charity towards one's neighbour.

Association to be broken off.

2. Choice of a definite point at which one's besetting sin is to be faithfully resisted.

3. Spiritual discipline:

A time for prayer every day.

A planned course of Bible-reading.

A liturgical service to be said.

Constant vigilance to maintain fellowship with Christ.

Thanksgiving

Act of Faith

Thanks be to you, O God, for the unspeakable gift of your mercy. I believe with all my mind that you have pardoned me and restored me to the first purity that was mine at baptism; I believe that you have washed me thoroughly with living water, and that you have buried me with Christ that I may rise again in him; I believe that what has been loosed on earth has been loosed in heaven, and that there is joy in heaven on my account.

Act of Hope

I hope with all my soul that you will keep me faithful to you until death, that you will grant me strength to carry out my resolutions, discipline to come back to confession when it is necessary, and that finally you will grant me to enter with all your saints into your Kingdom.

Prayer after Confession

I love you with all my heart, O God my Father,

because you always receive me, your prodigal son, with loving-kindness,

O Jesus Christ,

because you are a faithful Friend who give your life for me,

O Holy Ghost,

because your light and your fire never leave my heart in spite of my indifference.

Grant that I may love you more, and above all else, O beloved Saviour; that I may give up myself to your service and to the service of my brethren, seeking not my own but your glory, O God, Father, Son, and Holy Ghost, ever blessed. Amen.

Below we give another form of absolution, which is a prayer for pardon, inspired by the Greek Orthodox Liturgy.

Prayer for Absolution

℣. Lord Jesus Christ, you have accorded to Peter the forgiveness of sins after his repentance, and you have justified the publican who confessed his faults. Receive also the confession of your servant, and in your goodness pardon his sin, because you are a God of compassion, of mercy and of love for all men, and to you we render Glory together with the Father Eternal and the Holy Spirit of goodness and of life, now and forever.

℞. Amen.

Declaration of Forgiveness

℣. This is a faithful saying and worthy of all acceptation, that Christ Jesus came into the world to save sinners. Your faith has saved you, your sins are forgiven.

Act of Praise

Lord, you have called me,
    and the sound of your crying has pierced my deafness.
You have shone
    and the splendour of your glory has banished my
    blindness.
You have shed forth the perfume of your grace
    and breathing it I sigh for you.
I have tasted you
    and I hunger and thirst for you.
You have touched me
    and I burn with desire for your peace.

(After St Augustine).

141

CONCLUSION

SHORT EXHORTATION TO CONFESSION[1]

(from Martin Luther's *Great Catechism*)

CONCERNING confession, we have always taught that it must be free. . . .

Today, everyone knows all about that; unfortunately, there are many who know it only too well; they do what they like, and use their freedom as an excuse for never coming to confession again. It is easy to understand things that are pleasant, and the Gospel seems perfectly clear when it is being gentle. . . . Those who will neither believe nor live by the Gospel and fulfil their duties as Christians, are unworthy of its benefits. What would people say if you wanted to enjoy everything without it costing you any effort or expense? But it is not to those people that our preaching is addressed; we will not let them enjoy our liberty . . . For those among the people who will not obey the Gospel, it is necessary that there be a gaoler, to be for them the devil and executioner of God. As for the rest, who listen willingly to what is said to them, we do not cease preaching to them, warning them and arousing their zeal, so that they will not neglect such a precious and comforting treasure, offered them by the Gospel. It is in order to instruct and exhort the simple that we shall say also a few words about confession.

Apart from the confession of which we are speaking here, there are two sorts of confession. They might be termed general, and are common to all Christians. One of them consists in confession to God alone; the other, in confession to one's neighbour alone, and asking his forgiveness. Both are included in the Lord's Prayer, in

[1] This part is not found in the first edition of 1529. But in the same year Luther added it to the second edition.

which we say: 'Forgive us our trespasses, as we forgive them that trespass against us.' Indeed, the whole prayer is really a confession. What, in fact, does our prayer mean, but that we confess that we do not do what we ought to do, and that we ask for God's grace and the joy of a good conscience? Such confession ought to be made constantly all our lives, for it pertains to the Christian to recognize himself to be a sinner and to ask for grace.

The second of these two confessions, that which everyone owes to his neighbour, is also contained in the Lord's Prayer. We ought to confess to each other and forgive each other our trespasses, before coming to God and asking him to forgive us. We are all guilty in regard to one another; so we can—and even must—confess publicly, in front of all, and without false shame, for none is of more worth than another and none does his duty to God and to his neighbour. Apart from this general guilt, there is a particular guilt: when we have roused a brother to wrath, we are guilty in regard to him and ought to ask his forgiveness. Thus we have in the Lord's Prayer a double absolution: we have the remission of sins committed against God together with that of sins committed against our neighbour, on condition, however, that we forgive our neighbour and are reconciled with him.

Apart from this necessary daily public confession there is private confession, which is made to one brother. Its usefulness is this: when there is some especial weight upon our conscience, oppressing and tormenting us, when we cannot find serenity, and when we are not strong enough in the faith, we can then disburden ourselves to a brother, and seek from him, as often as we wish, counsel and consolation of a sort to strengthen us. Private confession is not rendered obligatory by any commandment, as are the two kinds of confession of which we have spoken above; on the contrary, each is free to use it when he feels the need of it. Christ, in fact, has put absolution in the mouth of his Christendom, and commanded it to loose us from our sins.[1] So when the heart is sorrowing for its sins and longs for consolation, it finds here a

[1] Matt. 18.15-19.

143

sure refuge, where it hears the Word of God, and learns that God, through the ministry of a man, looses and absolves it from its sins.

As I have often said, confession is composed of two parts. The first is our own act: we groan under the weight of our sins and we ask for consolation and comfort for our souls. The second is the act of God: by the word which he has placed in the mouth of man, he absolves me from my sins. This is the chief and most noble part, that which makes confession so sweet and consoling. Now, up to the present, the part which is our own act has alone been emphasized; that we should make a perfectly pure confession was alone considered important, and nothing was said of the other part, which nevertheless is the more necessary. Thus confession was represented as a good work, done to requite God; and we were told that if our confession was not of perfect exactitude the absolution was invalid and our sins were not forgiven. This was stressed to such a point that people were led to despair of being able to confess so purely, for the impossible was being asked. No man could calm his conscience by putting his trust in absolution. They have thus made our dear confession not only useless to us, but also harsh and bitter, to the great detriment and loss of souls.

Therefore it is necessary to distinguish very clearly the two parts of confession. We must consider our own action as of little account, and, conversely, we must attach the greatest importance to the Word of God. We must not go to confession in order to perform a good work and give something to God, but, on the contrary, to receive what he gives to us. You ought not to present yourself in order to enumerate your qualities or your faults. If you are a Christian, I know them already; if you are not, I know them still better. But what matters is that you should bewail your misery and seek help, in order to have once more a joyful heart and conscience.

No-one has the right to coerce you by commandments; but this is what we say: to every Christian, as to every man who would be a Christian, we here give the advice to go and seek the precious treasure contained in confession. . . . Anyone who does not go to confession of his own free will, to receive absolution, would do better to abstain from it. The same is true of anyone who goes to confession in order to perform a good work, however pure his confession. We exhort you, on the contrary, to confess and unveil your misery, not thereby to perform a meritorious act, but to hear the word which God wills should be addressed to you. This word or absolution, you must consider as a great and precious treasure, and receive it with respect and thankfulness.

If these things were explained, and it were shown how necessary confession is to us, there would be no need to use constraint; each would be urged on by his conscience, and would experience a fear from which he would be glad to be freed. If a poor miserable beggar heard that in a certain place were being distributed rich alms of money and clothing, would he need to be taken there by a policeman? He would run thither of his own accord, with all speed, so as not to arrive too late. But if all the beggars were ordered to gather in that place, without being told why, would they not go there unwillingly, without hoping to receive anything, but on the contrary loath to let their poverty and misery be seen? In the same way, if confession is made a law, nothing being said of the treasure enshrined in it, the only result is to turn people against it.

. . . As for us, we do not tell you to expose your stains so that we may see them as in a mirror, but we give you this counsel: if you are poor and in misery, go and confess, and use this means to health. He who grieves over his misery will experience the desire for it, and will betake himself to it joyfully. As for those who are indifferent, and who do not come of themselves, we leave them to act as they will—but let them know that we do not look upon them as Christians.

Thus we teach that confession is an excellent thing, precious and comforting, and we urge that no-one should despise such a benefit, whose full price our misery ought to make us feel. If you are a Christian, you will come on your own, without needing to be driven by me or constrained by the commandment of the Pope, and you will ask to share in this treasure. If, on the other hand, you despise it, and if you are too proud to confess your sins, we conclude that you are no Christian, and that neither ought you to share in the Sacrament. You despise, in fact, what no Christian ought to despise, and from that we see also that you despise the Gospel.

To sum up, we do not want any compulsion, but whoever does not heed our preaching and does not obey our exhortation, ought not to share in the benefits of the Gospel, and we do not wish to have anything in common with such a man. If you were a true Christian, in your joy you would be ready to go more than a hundred miles to win this treasure; you would not wait to be compelled, you would come of yourself and oblige us to give it you. This would be quite the opposite of what happens now; we confessors would be the ones to be constrained by God's commandment, whereas you would enjoy freedom. We force no-one; we approve, on the contrary, that we should be forced, just as we are forced to preach and to administer the sacraments.

So when I urge the practice of confession, I am but urging every man to be a Christian. If I succeed in bringing you to that, I shall at the same time have succeeded in bringing you to confession. For those who desire to become pious Christians, to be delivered from their sins and to have the joy of a good conscience, hunger and thirst truly, and eagerly seek the bread wherewith they may be filled, just as a hart when hunted and devoured by thirst seeks a cooling spring. 'Like as the hart desireth the water-brooks: so longeth my soul after thee, O God,' says Psalm 42.[1] That is to say, as a thirsty hart longs to find a cool spring, my soul thirsts for the Word of God, for absolution and the Sacrament. If it were explained in this way what confession is, it would come to be loved and desired; people would come flocking to it, and we should have more penitents than we wanted.

[1] Ps. 42.1.

LUTHER'S *LITTLE CATECHISM*[1]

What is Confession?

Confession comprises two things. Firstly, one must confess one's sins; secondly, one must receive absolution or pardon from the confessor as from God himself, and doubt not, but firmly believe, that by this means our sins are forgiven before God in Heaven.

What sins must be confessed?

Before God, we must accuse ourselves of every sin, even those of which we are unaware, as we do in the Lord's Prayer; but before the confessor we ought only to declare those sins which we know and feel in our hearts.

What are those sins?

Consider thy state according to the Ten Commandments, . . . and ask thyself if thou hast been disobedient, unfaithful, idle, wrathful, lustful, argumentative, if thou hast wronged anyone in word or in deed, if thou hast stolen, or if thou hast caused any harm by thy negligence or carelessness.

Show me, I beg thee, a short form of confession.

Thou shouldst say to the confessor:

'Dear and venerable master, I beg thee to hear my confession and to declare to me the remission of my sins for the love of God.'

Speak!

'I, a poor sinner, confess before God, that I am guilty of every sin . . .'

(A master or mistress should say:)

'Especially, I confess before thee that I have not faithfully brought up my family, my children, and my servants to the glory of God. I have sworn, and set a bad example by my unchaste words and deeds; I have done injury to my neighbour, I have

[1] Published by 'Je Sers', Paris, 1947, *Œuvres de Martin Luther*, 'Les Livres symboliques', pp. 36-8. An English translation is to be found in Wace and Buchheim, *Luther's Primary Works*, Hodder & Stoughton, London, 1896, pp. 15-16.

spoken ill of him, I have deceived him concerning the quality of the merchandise, and I have not given him all that was his due.' Let each add here what else he has done contrary to God's commandments and his state of life.

But if any does not feel himself burdened with similar or greater sins, let him not be anxious, let him not seek yet other sins or imagine them, turning confession into torture. Let him on the contrary limit himself to declaring one or two sins which he knows he has committed, and let him say: 'Especially, I confess that once I swore, uttered unchaste words, or was negligent', etc. . . . That suffices.

If *per impossibile* you do not feel yourself guilty of any sin, declare no especial sin, but receive forgiveness after the general confession which you make to God in the presence of the confessor.

Then the confessor shall say:

'God be merciful to you and strengthen your faith! Amen. Do you believe that my forgiveness is the forgiveness of God?

The penitent shall reply:

'Yes, dear master.'

And then the confessor shall say:

'According to your faith be it done unto you. And I, by the commandment of our Lord Jesus Christ, do forgive you your sins, in the Name of the Father, the Son, and the Holy Ghost. Amen. Go in peace.'

As for those whose conscience is sorely burdened and who are anguished and tormented, the confessor will know how to comfort them and reawaken their faith by various words from the Scriptures.

INDEX OF BIBLICAL REFERENCES